DISCOVERING EMBROIDERY

Round cushion in red and white linen appliqué.
By Winsome Douglass

DISCOVERING EMBROIDERY

by

WINSOME DOUGLASS

MILLS & BOON LIMITED
17–19 FOLEY STREET, LONDON W1A 1DR

First published 1955
Second impression 1955
Third impression 1956
Fourth impression 1958
Fifth impression 1961
Sixth impression 1965
Seventh impression 1968
Eighth impression 1971

S.B.N. 263 69981 1

Reproduced and Printed in Great Britain by
Redwood Press Limited, Trowbridge & London

FOREWORD

by Miss E. W. Thomson, Crafts Adviser and Instructor

"DISCOVERING EMBROIDERY" is a simple and fascinating text book on this absorbing subject handed down to us from very early times.

The author, an authority on her subject, puts forward the plea that through the knowledge of stitchery and an awareness of materials and colour, students at an early stage can master this exciting craft.

The beginner, having been given examples of stitchery from the very simple to the more advanced, will be able to proceed with confidence to work on her own. The instructions and illustrations on how to combine stitches, leading to the making of patterns, are so clearly given that, through the resulting experiments, her own creative powers will be released.

The problem of colour, which is so difficult for beginners, will be greatly simplified by the examples given. Suggestions for the making of delightful and useful articles which lend themselves to embroidery also form an important part of this book. Shapes with accurate measurements are given, so that there can be no doubt in the mind of the embroideress on how to proceed. The section on " finishings " is most valuable. This stage of the work is so often neglected, with the result that much otherwise good work is spoiled. The other suggestions for design are all constructive and will give confidence to the beginner to go ahead.

I gladly commend this most useful and inspiring book to all those who eagerly desire to take part in a craft which plays such an important part in our lives and which is a never-ending source of pleasure.

E. W. T.

Edinburgh

ACKNOWLEDGMENT

THE Author and publishers acknowledge with thanks the co-operation of Needlework Development Scheme, 89 Wellington Street, Glasgow, in kindly making available the photographs reproduced in the frontispiece and Plates 1, 2, 3, 4, 5 and 6.

CONTENTS

LIST OF PLATES

INTRODUCTION

SINCE the Stone Age, and probably before that, women have plied the needle both for pleasure and necessity. Here I would like to deal in a small way with the pleasure-giving side of sewing. Many people, I feel, need just a little help and encouragement to set them on the right road to creating their own embroidery designs. This is not as difficult as it may sound, and I hope that all who read this book will find something which will help them to fulfil the creative urge to design and make something beautiful.

I do not propose to deal with every aspect of embroidery, but I have tried to encourage and stimulate readers to make some of their own designs and to use a variety of stitches. I have not attempted to include every possible embroidery stitch, but have chosen some which I think will be most suitable for the contemporary style of stitching and design which the book illustrates.

Those who are beginners I hope will find the work simple and progressive, and those who are experienced with the embroidery needle I hope will also find something upon which to build and enlarge to their ultimate satisfaction.

First a word or two about tools. These are not many and are within everyone's scope to obtain. A selection of needles with large and small eyes—usually crewel needles, a large pair of cutting-out shears, a small pair of sharp-pointed scissors and a comfortably fitting thimble are necessary. Do not regard the thimble with disdain, for it plays an important part in the embroidery. The pushing-through action it has helps to get the rhythm of the stitch, and this in turn makes for even and smooth embroidery. It also prevents pricked and bleeding fingers which soil the work, and rough finger-ends which catch the thread and fray it.

When choosing your embroidery thread, make sure that it pulls easily through the material. If you have to tug it, and it looks ugly and ungainly on the fabric, it is too thick, and you should choose a thinner type of thread, or if it is of the stranded kind, use fewer strands. Use fairly short lengths when working, as this saves frayed and soiled cotton and knots which are always a bother to disentangle. Of course there are many varieties of thread available these days, and it is up to the embroideress herself to make a suitable choice, but I should advise a beginner to choose a firm, smooth thread—not too fine—to start with. As you become more skilled you can experiment with finer and more difficult cottons. Avoid the springy, slippery kind of thread that tangles when you look at it, or you spend all your time unknotting it, until in the end you become so irritated that you give up your work in despair.

Many people, fired with enthusiasm in the making of their first piece of embroidery, tackle things that are much too big—and you all know the story of the discarded piece of work that has become too boring to finish. Start by really learning some of the stitches, and try them out on a piece of firm fabric with a large needle and thread. In no time at all you will feel sufficiently competent to tackle successfully your piece of embroidery.

One more word about needles. The size of the needle is important too. It should make a hole in the fabric large enough to pull the thread through without tugging, but not so large that it leaves a gaping hole.

Now as to fabrics. Of course there is an almost unlimited choice, but do try to choose a fabric that is really suitable for the purpose for which it is to be used. For instance, if your article is to be laundered frequently, then choose a washable material, one that does not shrink and has fast colour. If the article is not to be washed, your field of choice is much greater, but again think of the function of the piece of embroidery, and choose accordingly. For the beginner I recommend a firm, smooth, evenly woven cotton fabric which will launder and iron well, and not slip about when you are working it. For young children felt is an ideal material, as there are no threads to fray out and it keeps its shape well. They need, too, a stout, short needle with a large eye, and a fairly thick cotton which is not stranded.

As well as felts and cottons, of course, we can use woollen material. This often makes extremely attractive embroideries, but needs a little more care in handling. It has a warm, cosy effect, and cushions in particular look very well made up in woollen fabric. The silks, satins and organdies need quite a high degree of skill and often must be worked in a frame in order to keep their shape.

When cutting out rectangular shapes it is essential to cut by the thread of the material, so that when the article is finished the edges will be straight. Often this can be facilitated by drawing a thread and cutting by this. This is a useful method, too, for laying hems, and ensures their being perfectly straight. You will find that this method is well worth the time spent on it, and the finished work will have a higher degree of neatness, and be as near perfection as possible. I should perhaps stress this idea of perfection now. At all times care and neatness are essential in embroidery. Even the most simple processes need to be done well, and perfection should be the aim of the embroideress. In actual fact this takes no more time than something that is badly done and has to be taken out. By the way, if you should need to take some stitchery out—as we all do sometimes—the best method is to cut it out carefully and throw away the pieces of thread. In this way great holes are not left in the material, and one is not tempted to use again a dirty and frayed piece of thread.

It is advisable to tack down all hems before working, and often the shape of the piece of work is best tacked on to the fabric too. For instance, when working a rectangular table mat or a round cushion, tack round the outside of the paper shape, and only remove tackings when the article is finished.

There are several methods of transferring designs on to material, but as a rule two are sufficient for the majority of embroideresses. If the fabric is smooth and firm—such as cotton or linen and sometimes silk—the use of wax transferring paper is best. Place the design on the material and slip the transferring paper between the two, pinning down so that none of them slips about, and then go firmly over the lines with a stylo or sharp, hard pencil. Wax transferring paper can be obtained in several colours—blue, black and red for light-coloured fabrics, and white and yellow for the darker ones. The colour from some paper does come off on to the thread, but as a rule this washes out when laundered.

The other method for transferring designs on to material is used mainly for woollen fabrics and those with a rough surface which do not take paper transfers easily. This method—tacking—takes much longer, but is clear and lasting. The design is placed over the material and tacked firmly round the edge. Next trace over all the lines with small running stitches going right through both paper and fabric. When all the design has been completed, tear off the paper; the lines of stitching show up the pattern. When working in the embroidery cotton, sew directly over the running stitches, and if these show afterwards, they can easily be clipped out.

The following pages will, I hope, encourage the embroideress to try to make her own designs. I have tried to keep the instructions simple and easy for you to follow, even if you have no gift for drawing. Of course, the time comes when some drawing is necessary, and if you are one of those who cannot hold a pencil the right way up and have to buy your designs for embroidery, I hope this book will help you to choose those designs which are suitable. In the main, choose well-spaced designs without too much detail, so that there is plenty of scope to use your sense of stitchery. Many of the designs try to impose a certain stitch on the embroideress by virtue of their crowded and close quality. Keep to firm shapes, and see that the shape of the whole design fits suitably on to the article on which it is to be used.

Many embroideries done today depend largely on a neat and skilful repetition of one stitch, and endeavour to create almost a photographic reproduction of flowers or birds or other objects. I feel that this is not true embroidery, and the embroideress who does this type of work loses much of the sense of creation that she should have if she employed all the skills of stitchery at her disposal. By skilful use of stitches, bearing in mind their shapes and thicknesses, one is able to suggest different textures and patterns which are infinitely more interesting to work and look at.

However simple a stitch is, it has a beauty of its own, and these stitches combined in countless different ways can give a sense of beauty and vitality that is never present in a mere mechanical repetition of the same stitch.

You will find illustrated a few of the simpler stitches which can be used to make delightful embroideries, but the embroideress must use her own ingenuity and creative power in order to achieve something beautiful. Many of these stitches, no doubt, you learned at school, but perhaps the illustrations that follow will refresh your memory.

When starting off your embroidery, put in a few running stitches in the opposite direction from the line of work. This is quite secure, and saves ugly knots in the back of the material. To finish off, take the needle through to the back of the work and slip it back through some of your stitches. When moving from one line to another, do not carry the thread along the back unless the distance is very small. A much neater finish is obtained by finishing off and starting again.

Nearly all these stitches which are illustrated are flat, firm ones. They can be washed and ironed quite safely without the thread being disturbed by the washing or caught up with the iron.

Note.—Since the above was written, the makers of Simplicity Patterns have produced a dressmaker's tracing paper, in three colours, which will transfer designs satisfactorily on to most smooth fabrics, including the finer felts.

SIMPLE STITCHES

Running stitch (1)

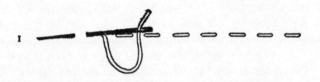

This is the simplest stitch, but extremely useful. There are quite a number of ways of threading and whipping it. You can see a few illustrated, but there are many more which no doubt you can try out for yourself.

Whipped running (2, 3)

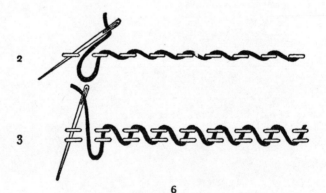

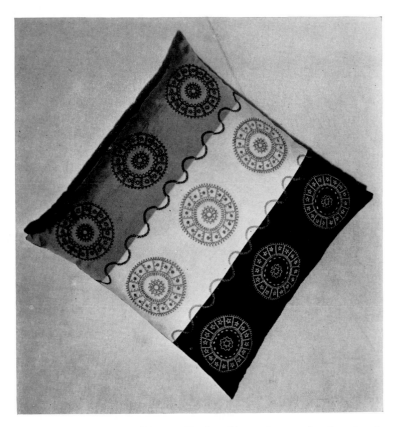

PLATE I.—*Striped cushion in black, white and grey showing simple circular motifs. By Winsome Douglass*

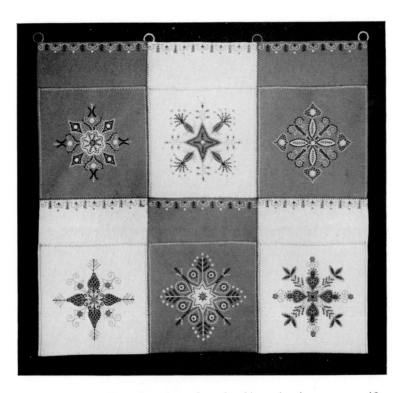

PLATE 2.—*Wall pockets in red and white, showing star motifs.*
By Winsome Douglass

This is a line of running stitch with a contrasting thread whipped over it. The needle does not pass through the material, but comes down through the running stitch each time. Take care not to get the tension too tight. A nicely curved stitch is best.

Threaded running (4, 5)

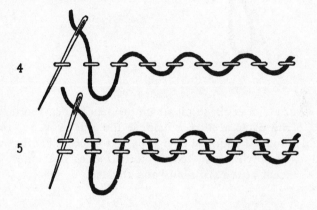

A line of running stitch with a contrasting thread going up through one stitch and down through the next without passing through the material. Again the tension is important. In the double rows of whipped and threaded running it is essential that the running stitches are exactly underneath each other.

Chain stitch (6)

—is another easy stitch, and is made by taking up a small piece of fabric with the thread under the needle. When making the second stitch, insert the needle into the same hole where the thread came out.

Whipped chain (7)

—is a variety of chain stitch which produces a firm, cord-like effect. A row of chain stitch is made in the usual way, and then a second thread is whipped over it by putting the needle down behind each stitch. The second thread does not enter the material except at the beginning and the end.

Zig-zag chain (8)

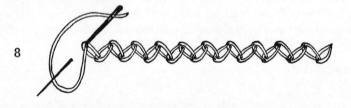

—makes a softer line than the firm, straight chain. It is merely the ordinary chain worked on the slant, but when making the second and subsequent stitches the needle must pierce the thread of the previous loop. This is in order to ensure that the stitch lies quite flat.

Detached chain (9)

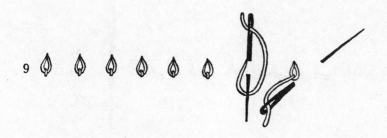

This, I think, explains itself. It is merely an ordinary chain stitch which is fastened down by inserting the needle into the material just below the loop.

Magic chain (10)

—is perhaps a little more complicated, but nevertheless can be mastered in a short time. The needle is threaded with two contrasting threads. The method is the same as that for ordinary chain stitch, except that first one coloured thread is placed under the needle when making the stitch, and then the other alternately along the line. The thread not under the needle is left loose. If a little of the wrong colour shows on the surface, a slight tug of the thread will cause it to disappear. Of course different sequences of stitches may be used: for instance, three dark to one light and so on.

Buttonhole stitch (11)

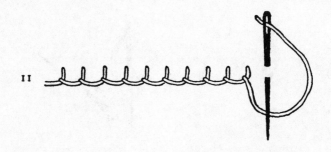

11

This simple stitch is a basis for an infinite variety of stitches and fillings. It is worked by inserting the needle into the material vertically and bringing the point out in the line of work with the thread under the needle. The working is from left to right. The spacing between the stitches can be varied: for instance, two or three stitches worked closely and then a space gives another effect. When worked very closely, with all the stitches lying side by side, this stitch is used for cut work, buttonhole bars and scalloping.

Whipped buttonhole stitch (12)

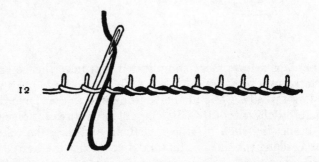

12

This is the same as the previous stitch, with a second thread whipped over the horizontal stitch without passing through the material, as in whipped running and whipped chain.

Vandyke buttonhole (13)

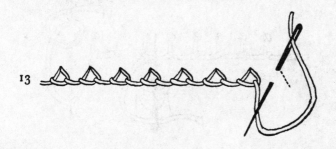

13

This is a most attractive stitch, and is based on the ordinary buttonhole.   The method of working is exactly the same, except that the needle is sloped from right to left when making the first stitch.   It is then inserted in the same hole at the top and sloped from left to right—making a triangular stitch.   It is important to remember that the thread must always be kept under the needle.

Crossed buttonhole stitch (14)

14

This is similar to the previous stitch of vandyke buttonhole. This time, instead of inserting the needle in the same hole as you did to make the point, take it a little beyond, so that the threads will cross.   Some care is needed to get this stitch quite even and regular.

Knotted buttonhole stitch (15)

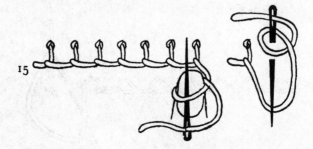

This stitch is perhaps the most difficult of the buttonhole group, but it is quite a useful stitch.   Bring the needle through from the back of the material, loop the thread round the thumb and slip the needle through it.   Then slip the loop off the thumb and with the needle still in the loop take up a piece of material as in ordinary buttonhole stitch.   Before drawing the needle through the material, pull the thread so that the loop is tightened and forms the knot at the top of the stitch.

Couching (16*a* and *b*)

Couching is another simple stitch which has many varieties. Some of them are illustrated here, but the embroideress can devise many more.   It is worked by laying one or two or several threads along the line of work and stitching over them at intervals.

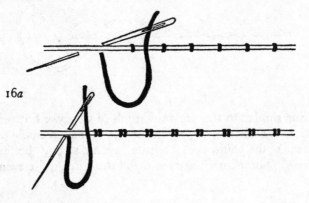

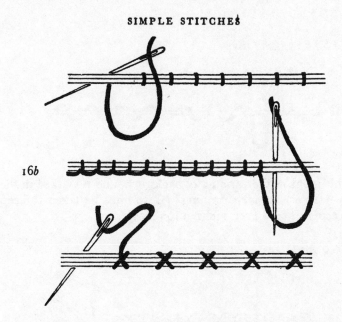

16*b*

This stitch can be a short, straight stitch or any of the stitches already learned, such as buttonhole. Cross stitch, which is dealt with later in this book because of its special uses (p. 109), is also suitable. The underneath thread must be firm, while the tying-down stitch must be taut and even.

Backstitch (17)

17

This line stitch, worked from right to left, is made by bringing the needle out a short distance along the line to be worked. It is then put in again at the beginning of the line and brought out an equal distance beyond the first hole. The needle must always go back into the same hole made by the previous stitch.

Threaded backstitch (18)

This is one of the varieties of backstitch, and is worked in the same way as threaded running. Care must be taken to keep the second thread even and not too loose.

Pekinese stitch (19)

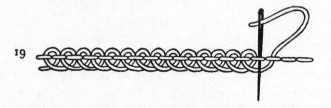

This is worked with a contrasting thread on to a line of backstitch. It is worked from left to right, bringing the needle up through the second stitch and back down through the first stitch, proceeding on up through the third and down through the second stitch.

Coral knot (20)

Coral knot is another very useful line stitch, and is particularly good for going round rather intricate lines. It is made by taking up a small piece of material, and the thread being placed first over the needle and then under it, thus forming a small knot. This is repeated at short intervals along the line.

Zig-zag coral (21)

This is, of course, based on the previous stitch and worked in a zig-zag fashion. The left-hand stitch is worked as for ordinary

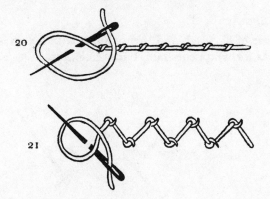

coral knots, but for the right-hand stitch the thread must be looped as in the diagram. Hold the loop down with the thumb and insert the needle into the loop after raising the thumb.

Fly stitch (22)

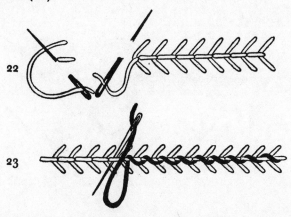

This stitch can be worked open or closed, depending on the effect desired. Bring the needle through from the back of the material and put it in the fabric a little way along the line of work, bringing it out again sloping upwards to the left. Next place it in the material on the right of the line level with the left-hand stitch and bring it out of the hole made on the line of work, with the thread under the needle.

Whipped fly stitch (23)

Make a line of fly stitch and then whip it with a contrasting thread just as for whipped chain, buttonhole, etc.

Single fly stitch (24)

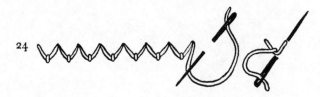

This stitch is worked from left to right, and is based on a **V**. Bring the needle out at the top of the left arm and insert it exactly opposite at the top of the right arm, bringing the needle out at the bottom of the **V** and keeping the thread under the needle.   Tie the loop down with a small stitch at the base.

Chain and fly stitch (25)

This is a combination of two stitches.   Make a chain stitch first and then an ordinary fly stitch, taking care to use the holes of the previous chain stitch when making the following one. This stitch can be done separately and makes an attractive filling (26).   When the stitch has been made, chain and then fly, tie the loop down with a small stitch at the base.

BORDERS AND MOTIFS

Now that these stitches and their variations have been mastered, one can try out some borders. These can be very attractive and are quite easily built up. Often a single line of stitching looks thin and hard, but with the addition of one or two other stitches it can be transformed into something beauti-

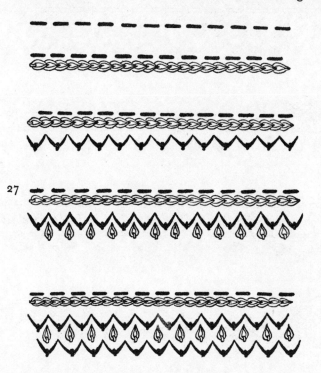

ful and rich-looking. There is an illustration (27) starting with a running stitch and showing how a rich-looking border can be developed. Chain, single fly and detached chain have been added to the running stitch, and finally another row of single fly stitch. Each of these borders is attractive in itself, and the number of stitches you use depends on the weight and thickness of the border required. Care must be taken with the position of the stitching, as a line too far away or too close to the previous one can completely alter the effect. After all, if a border is to be made, the stitches must look as though they belong to one another. Notice, too, how the lines of detached chain fit in to the single fly stitch in a regular manner.

You will find, too, several other borders. The first (28) has

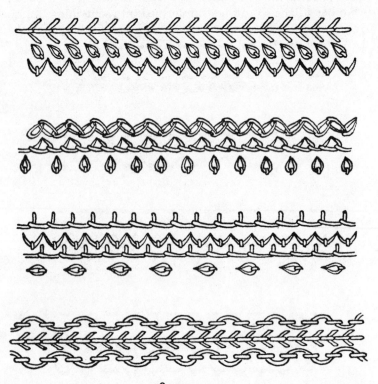

28, 29, 30, 31

fly stitch, detached chain fitting in to the slope of the fly stitch and then a row of single fly stitch, also keeping regular with the detached chain. Next (29) we have zig-zag chain, vandyke buttonhole and detached chain stitch. The third border (30) has buttonhole, single fly, buttonhole again, and then a row of detached chain done horizontally. The next one (31) has two rows of threaded running exactly regular with each other and a line of fly stitch down the centre.

We then have some more complicated borders (32, 33, 34), but still using the same stitches. The embroideress can devise many more for her pleasure, and can make them into thick and

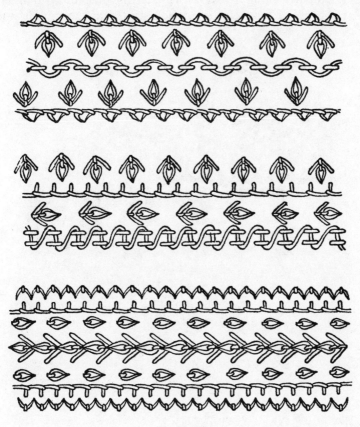

32, 33, 34

rich lines of stitching. Using her ingenuity in the combining of stitches, she will soon feel the satisfaction of creation, and from this beginning can move on to develop a sense of design.

The simplest form of making a motif is to use your stitches in circles. These can be drawn in varying sizes with a compass or even round a jar, and by combining your stitches as you did when making the borders you can get very attractive results. The motifs can be as tiny as the top of a pincushion or as large as the top of a cushion-cover. Try starting them off with different centres—a knot of chain stitch started in the middle and

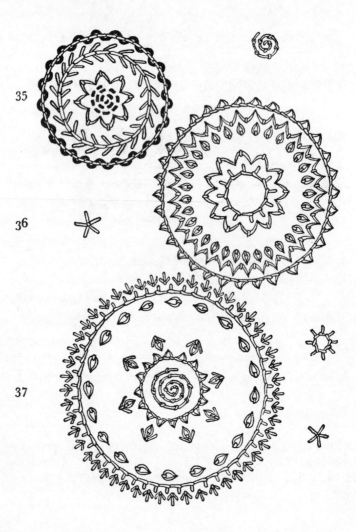

worked round and round like a snail-shell, or a circle of button-hole—and just see what pretty effects you can obtain. There are illustrated three different-sized circles. The first (35) consists of running stitch, single fly, continuous fly and threaded backstitch. The second (36) has buttonhole, single fly, detached chain, single fly and vandyke buttonhole. Finally the largest (37) combines coral knot, vandyke buttonhole, detached chain and fly, detached chain, buttonhole and fly stitch. When making your circular motifs, try working the circles at varying distances from each other. Thus you may get a solid centre with a space and then a thick border, and so on.

From there we can go on to make little four-pointed stars—still using stitchery and without drawing. The beginning is the same—with a central spot of stitching. The four arms can then be developed on the same lines as the border stitching and other

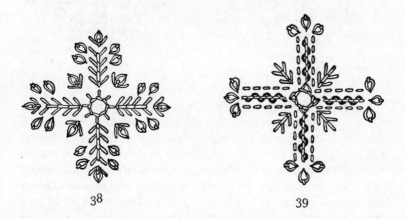

38   39

groups of stitchery introduced into the four spaces. The first (38) has been started with a circle of buttonhole stitch, and arms of fly stitch added with detached chain, and chain and fly at the ends, and single chain and fly stitches added to the spaces. The next one (39) has a centre of vandyke buttonhole and arms of threaded backstitch, bordered by running stitch with detached chain on the ends and short stalks of fly stitch in the spaces.

The third one (40) has a circle of rather close buttonhole stitch, with arms made of two rows of buttonhole worked back to back and then whipped together. A small fly and chain stitch is on the end of the arm and a small circle of buttonhole in the space. The fourth star (41) starts with a knob of chain stitch worked round and round from the centre, the arms are of buttonhole and single fly and then a row of running stitch encloses the arms, with detached chain in the spaces.

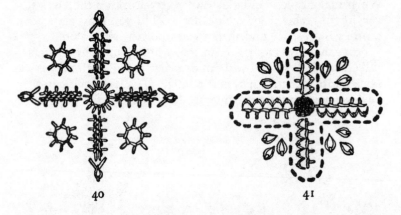

40   41

Many embroidery designs contain leaf and flower shapes. Only too often, however, they are small and crowded; but if you come across an open bold design that gives some scope for stitchery, try out some of your stitches to give different patterns within the leaf shapes. Opposite are illustrated some leaves, ordinary in outline but with varying use of embroidery stitches. This use of stitchery gives a much more vivid and lively piece of work and sustains interest for longer than the monotonous and mechanical working of satin stitch. Of course these are only a few of the many ways in which a creative embroideress can employ her stitchery.

You will see, too, a simple flower shape (45–7) illustrated in the same way as the leaves. By judicious use of stitch one can obtain either a bold, strong effect, as with firm straight stitches like chain, or a more delicate and lighter tone, as with vandyke buttonhole and fly stitch. With practice the beginner can soon acquire a sense of the fitness of the stitch for the shape it is to fill.

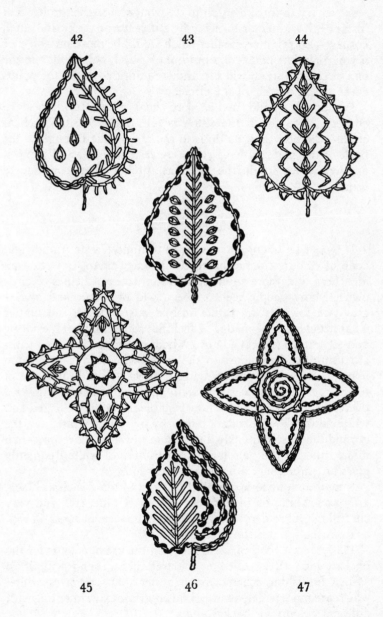

Never try to force a stitch to do what seems alien to it. For instance, it is difficult to make fly stitch turn narrow and small corners—a straighter, smaller stitch would be more suitable; or if you make the points of a buttonhole stitch point to the inside of a circle, the stitch will slip and look untidy—make the points come to the outside of the circle.

Perhaps I should say a word here about turning sharp corners. Usually, if the stitch is one likely to slip—such as chain—the best thing to do is to put the needle through to the back of the material as if you were fastening off, and bring it out again just inside the previous stitch. Then continue as usual.

COLOUR SCHEMES

It would be wrong for me to try to impose a strict and rigid code of colour schemes on to the needlewoman, but often an idea here and there stimulates one to invent schemes of one's own. Many people seem to be afraid of colour and always gravitate towards the rather insipid pastel shades, no matter what article is to be made. I feel that something bold, exciting and adventurous is called for. Vividness can be achieved without using all the colours in the rainbow. In fact, to use too many colours gives just as bad an effect as the insipid use of them. Strong contrasts look well, and sharpness of line gives a lively effect. We all know how well black and white or red and white look. People often fight shy of using white, on the ground that it soils quickly, but it is no worse in this respect than many other of the pale tones, and the use of white frequently gives an embroidery a light and lively look.

Sometimes one feels the need to work in tones such as black, grey and white, or in different shades of blue, etc., and very charming embroidery can result from this use of tones as well as from the use of strong contrasts.

This seems a good place to mention the use of colours for the background. Very often a coloured background will fit in with a furnishing scheme much better than cream or white, which are more widely used. I do advocate experimenting with different colours for backgrounds.

Really beautiful embroideries can be executed with the use of one colour only on a contrasting fabric. For instance, white embroidery on blue can look charming. In a case like this, of course, much depends on the variety and execution of the stitchery—in fact all the appeal of the embroidery is lodged in the skilful and sensitive use of stitch and design.

It is advisable for beginners to limit their colours to a few consisting of a light, a dark and perhaps one or two medium tones. A good idea is to choose three or four colours and to do your embroidery in these colours only, and resist the temptation to add a bit of this or a bit of that. In this way one can very soon achieve the clear, sharp, lively quality that many embroideries lack, and avoid the dull, tired and weary look, to say nothing of the confusion and jazziness, of those which one so often sees.

As well as experimenting with colour schemes, I suggest you try a little experimenting with the materials themselves. Sometimes a striped tea-cosy or cushion fits in with a colour scheme; or a piece of contrasting colour applied along the hem of a curtain gives the desired effect.

Section VI of this book deals with actual patchwork, but here I want to say a little about the joining of materials. The usual method is to machine the pieces together on the wrong side and then press open the seam. One need not stop at that, however, and here the use of embroidered borders comes in. To avoid an uninteresting seam, the join can be decorated with stitchery on each side so that in the end the join becomes a thing of beauty, as in the striped tea-cosy and tray-cloth which are illustrated (54–6). In fact, in some embroideries this can be the only decoration. So do not be afraid of joining your different materials together and using your knowledge of stitchery to make them attractive. When seaming two pieces of fabric together, make sure that they are both on the same grain of the material, and join them by the thread of the material. This is really important for a finished and perfect piece of work.

Another method, suitable for joining materials which do not fray, such as felt, is by fishbone stitch, which makes a flat seam.

c

This stitch is illustrated in the second group of stitches (p. 42) and can also be worked with a little space between the stitches (diagram 153, p. 106).

When a piece of embroidery is complete it usually needs pressing. I have found that the best method is to press over a damp cloth on the wrong side. Do see that all seams, hems, etc., are pressed as the work goes on. If you leave them all until the end they are often difficult to manage, and one finds oneself pressing in creases that should never be there.

Having discussed simple stitches, fabrics, colours, joinings and the simplest methods of designing with stitchery, I would now like to suggest some of the things you can make using these motifs. Of course these are only suggestions, and the embroideress herself can adapt the measurements and designs to fit her own needs. They are not meant to be slavishly copied, but to stimulate the needlewoman to create her own designs and patterns. Most of the patterns illustrated in this first section are based on shapes that are simple to cut—squares, rectangles and circles.

Pincushions

You will find four pincushions illustrated, but of course, as I have said before, they are only suggestions. A pincushion is quite a good thing to start with, although it does require a degree of skill and neatness.

Choose some small pieces of fabric and your coloured threads. For the round one (48) draw two circles 2″ in diameter and a long strip 1″ by 6¾″ on a piece of firm paper—drawing-paper does very well. Then cut out your fabric from these patterns, allowing ½″ turning all round. Next fold the material over the paper, keeping the edge firm and free from folds, and tack it through on to the paper. Tacking on to the paper will keep the shape of the circle and give quite a good finish to the pincushion. When you have tacked all your pieces of cloth on to the paper, draw in your design. If it is to be of circles, use different sizes, such as a thimble and a cotton-reel. When marking round the strip see that the spots come at equidistant intervals. Then work your design. Stitch up by neatly seaming the short edges of the strip on the wrong side and then seam

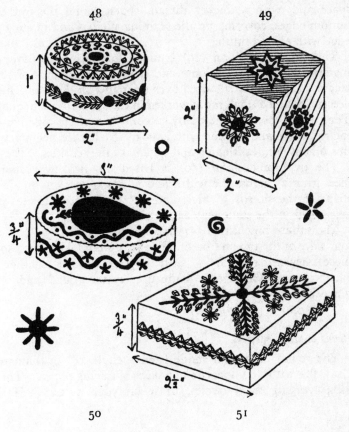

it carefully to the base of the pincushion on the right side. By the way, the base should have on it some small piece of embroidery to give a final finished touch. Before putting the top on, cut a circle of stiff card to put in the bottom to form a firm base for the pincushion. Now seam on the top, leaving a space for stuffing. When stuffing put in a little kapok at a time and stuff right down into the bottom seam. You will find that quite a lot of kapok is needed, but do put it in in small amounts, to avoid lumpiness. When it is packed firmly, seam up the space and, with a thicker thread, couch round the top and bottom edges, covering up the seaming stitches and making an edge with a good finish.

The cube pincushion (49) is made from six 2″ squares of material, using three colours and having two squares of each colour. The fabric is tacked over the paper in the way I have described, and a small motif worked in the centre of each square. The cube is then assembled by stitching the pieces together on the right side and stuffing with kapok. No card is necessary in this pincushion, as it can stand on any of the six sides.

The oval pincushion (50) is based on two oval shapes measuring 2″ across the width and 3″ along the length. The strip for the side is $\frac{3}{4}$″ high and $8\frac{1}{2}$″ long. It is made and assembled in the same way as the circular one.

The square pincushion (51) has measurements of $2\frac{1}{2}$″ on all four sides of the top and base. The strip round is made in four pieces measuring $2\frac{1}{2}$″ by $\frac{3}{4}$″, and they are seamed together at each corner. This too is made up like the round and oval pincushions.

Round cushion (52)

The round cushion is made from a circle 18″ in diameter. Draw this with a compass on to a piece of tracing paper. Then, using varying sized circles, draw on your pattern. If the

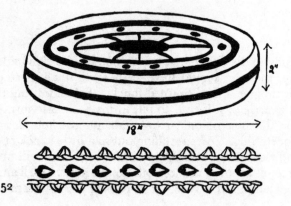

52

cushion is made in linen or firm fabric, the design can be put on with transfer paper, but if it is woolly material, tack through the paper with running stitches and then tear it off. Be sure to leave at least $\frac{1}{2}''$ turning right round the shape, and mark the edge of the circle with running stitches. Make a similar piece for the back, but this time only a small motif is necessary for the centre. The gusset is a straight $2''$ strip long enough to fit right round. You may have to join this with machine stitching, but be sure to press open the seam on the wrong side. When you have worked out your embroidery design, press each piece carefully on the wrong side and then sew them together, leaving a wide opening on the under-side to take the cushion pad. This opening can be invisibly slip-stitched together after the pad has been inserted. The pad itself can be made from calico cut slightly larger in size than the cushion itself. This is to ensure a good fit and a firm outline to the cushion. Fill the pad with kapok and put it inside the cushion-case.

Striped cushion (53)

53

The original cushion was made of a white, black and grey stripe with circular motifs worked in the same colours. The stripes measured 5″ by 15″ when finished. Cut them ½″ larger all round and work your motifs as described for making circles. I suggest black and white embroidery on the grey stripe, grey and white on the black stripe and black and grey on the white stripe, which incidentally is the central one. Machine the stripes together and press open the seams. The back is made from one piece of black fabric 15″ square with one of the motifs worked in the middle. Do not forget to leave your ½″ turning right round. The four gusset pieces, which can be different colours—say two grey and two white—each measure 15″ by 2″ (again, add turnings). They are embroidered with spots of chain stitch evenly spread along the middle. Machine the gusset pieces to the top of the cushion-case and then to three sides of the back. Machine up the corners and carefully press in the folds of the cushion. The case can be made from calico, cut slightly larger to give a firm outline to the cushion, and this can be filled with kapok. Be quite generous with the kapok to give a nice plump cushion. When the pad has been put in the case, turn in the edges and slip stitch together.

Tea-cosy (54–5)

The tea-cosy which is illustrated consists of a washable cover and a separate pad. The cover is made from pieces of different-coloured material machined together and then embroidered along the seams, both to emphasise the striped effect and to make a decorative join. This actual one was made from blue and white stripes—one blue on either side of a central white piece. Make the pattern by drawing a rectangle measuring 12″ by 9″ and then round off the corners. Join your pieces of material and then cut them to the tea-cosy shape, leaving ½″ turning all round. Press the seams open and then work your embroidery, using the stitches you have learned so far. The spots are worked in the same stitches, starting with a simple chain stitch spot at the top and gradually adding new stitches until the bottom motif is quite large. When you have finished the embroidery, machine the two sides of the tea-cosy together

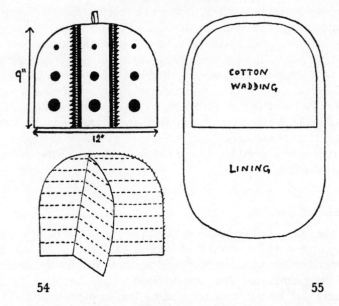

on the wrong side, taking care to match the stripes exactly. If you wish to have a loop for picking up the cosy (and this is a good idea), seam together a small strip of material and tack it in position before you machine the two sides together. This type of washable cover, I think, is better with a thin lining of lawn or similar fabric, so next make a cosy from this. Put it inside the first one, wrong sides together, and after turning in the lower edge of both the lawn cover and the embroidered one, slip stitch them together.

A loose pad can be made to go inside this cover, and is made in the following way. You will need some cotton wadding and material for lining. Often a contrasting colour can be attractive, and it can be cotton, just as the outside is. Cut two tea-cosy shapes in the wadding. Next cut two tea-cosy shapes, in *double* material with the fold at the bottom and allowing $\frac{1}{2}''$ turning on the curved edge, in the lining material (55). Fold this round each of the cotton-wool shapes, turn in the edges and tack round. Next rule lines along the shapes, and with one of your coloured threads embroider along the lines, taking care to make both back and front alike. The simplest form, of course, is running stitch, but much more elaborate forms of making the pad can be devised. For instance, it may be fastened down with straight stitches forming a star and worked at even intervals, or you may have a running stitch in a zig-zag or a looped line. Another alternative is to make knobs of solid chain stitch. This embroidered lining is essential to make a finished and perfect specimen, so do take care to finish it off and make it equal in beauty with the outside cover. When both pieces have been embroidered, press lightly and seam the curved edges together, taking care to pick up all the edges of the material.

Tray-cloth (56)

The tray-cloth is made to match the tea-cosy with a white main piece and 3″ border of blue at each end. See that the material is cut by the thread, and pull a thread for the turnings to make sure that they are straight. Cut the piece for the centre 14″ by 14″ and hem along two opposite edges. The pieces for the borders are 7″ by 14″, which is twice the width that they will be when finished, plus turnings. Make a line of tacking down the centre. Embroider the small spot motifs, to match the tea-cosy, on one side of the tacking, and then machine the strips on to the main piece. Press the seam towards the outside and then fold over the extra material to the back by the tacking stitches. Turn in the ends and the long edge over the raw edges of the seam and slip stitch together. This hides the raw seam and the back of the embroidery and keeps it neat.

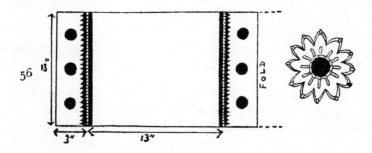

There are illustrated some other ways of joining material together to make up gay and attractive tea-cosies. The first (57) was in yellow with a grey strip along the bottom, and the other side a counter-change of grey top and yellow strip. The lining was black. Here you can make use of both your border stitches and leaf shapes. The embroidery was worked in white, yellow, grey and black.

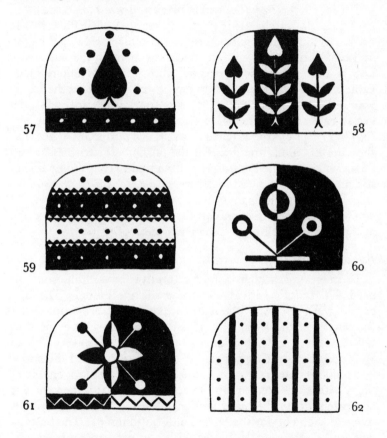

The second (58) was made in red and white stripes, again using the leaf shapes and having white embroidery on the red ground and red on the white. Again the lining was of black material.

The third suggestion (59) is for a horizontally striped cosy. Seam your pieces together before cutting the shape, as you did for the first cosy. Use embroidery stitches to decorate the joins, and solid spots of chain stitch along the stripes. This cosy was made in stripes of turquoise and white cotton material and worked in the same coloured threads. The lining was of white material.

The fourth tea-cosy (60) was in black and white, and the motif based on the circles which were illustrated earlier on in the book. White stitchery was used on the black side of the cosy and black on the white. The back was made in the same way, but so that when the two sides were joined together, black came next to white and white next to black. Here the lining was in yellow. The fifth (61) has four pieces to each side. Great care must be taken to ensure accurate joins. The last (62) has strips of tape stitched down at even intervals. See that the tape lies along the grain of the fabric. It can be fastened down with a simple embroidery stitch and perhaps some line of stitching worked down the centre.

These are simple forms of tea-cosies and later on (pp. 133 ff.) you will find methods of making further decoration, such as cords and pipings, which often enhance a piece of work.

Belt with pocket (63)

To make this, which is most attractive for a child, you will need felt, tailor's canvas and some silk for lining. The belt can be worn with or without the pocket. Cut two strips of felt the length of the waist plus 2″ and 2″ wide. Cut a piece of tailor's canvas the same length but slightly narrower. Make your design on tracing paper. A good idea is to fold the paper into sections and draw your flower, leaf or circle motif on one of them with a few connecting lines if necessary, and then trace it accurately on to the other sections. Do not forget to leave a space at each end for the button and buttonhole. The button-hole end I think looks better with the corners rounded off. Tack your design on to the felt by running through the paper and then tearing it off. Choose two or three colours and embroider the motifs quite thickly and firmly. Next slip stitch the tailor's canvas to the wrong side, so that the stitches do not

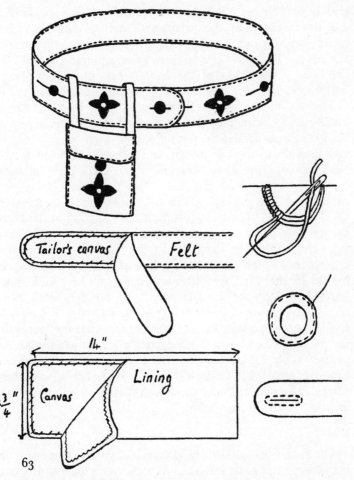

show through. Place the other piece of felt on the back and
stitch the front and lining together with a running stitch. This
can be whipped if necessary, or you could use an overcasting
stitch, using one of your embroidery cottons. Cut a slit through
the felt for the buttonhole and make a running stitch round it
to hold the felt together. The felt does not fray, but if the belt
is made in a fabric which does, then the buttonhole must be
worked with a buttonhole stitch. To make the button
take either a small circle of cardboard or a linen button and

pad it on top with a little cotton-wool. Cut a circle of felt slightly larger than the cardboard and, placing it and the wadding in the middle of the felt, run a gathering thread round the edge. Pull this up as tightly as possible and fasten off on the back. The front of the button can be embroidered to correspond with the belt and then stitched into position.

The pocket is a piece of felt measuring 14″ by 4¾″. Cut this piece out in tracing paper and round off the corners at one end. Fold the paper so that the pocket measures 5¾″ and the flap 2½″, and then draw on your design, using the motifs from the belt. Embroider in the same way and stitch on a piece of tailor's canvas as you did for the belt. Cut the lining ½″ bigger all round than the pocket. Turn this in and tack to the wrong side. Fold the pocket into position and, starting at the bottom corner and using a running stitch, sew up the side, stitching right through to the back, round the flap and then down the other side. Finally stitch across the top of the pocket. Make a button in the same way as you did for the belt and make a buttonhole loop for the fastening. To do this, work two or three loops of thread in the centre of the flap part of the pocket, trying them round the button to make sure that the loop will fit snugly, and then work a close buttonhole stitch round these strands. The loops which fasten the pocket to the belt are made from two strips of felt each 4½″ long. These are lined with felt, stitched with the running stitch and then seamed neatly to the back of the top of the pocket.

Wall pockets

These can be made to hold booklets, cards or specimens in the classroom, or can be useful in a bedroom for a brush, comb or slippers, etc. Those in the illustration (64) are for shoes. If you use felt no turnings are necessary, but if cotton material is used you must allow ½″ turnings along all edges. Measure your shoe and fold the material so that it shows for about 1½″ above the shoe at the back and the pocket comes about two-thirds of the way up. Allow ½″ play on each side of the shoe so that the fit is not too tight. Next tack in the lines along which you will machine when you come to divide the material into the individual pockets. Either tack or trace on your design.

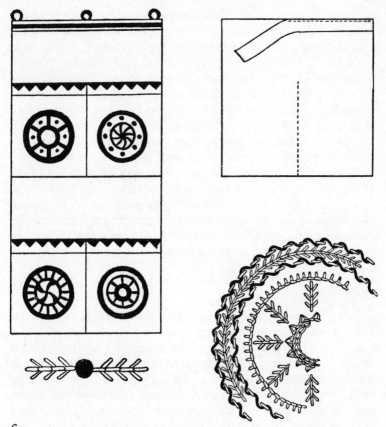

64

In the case of the pockets in the illustration, circular motifs
were used and borders combined from different embroidery
stitches. These were worked before the pockets were assembled.
If you are using felt, machine a piece of straight binding along
the top and the top of the pockets. This is to give strength
to the edges and to prevent stretching. When you have done
that, machine the two ends of the pockets, and the divisions.
This machine stitching can be covered by an embroidery
stitch, and extra stitches can be worked along each side of it to
give added decoration. The same method is applied when
making the pockets of cotton fabric, except that the tape must

be stitched on the right side first and then folded over to the back and stitched down. This is just like an ordinary facing. The two ends of the pockets must be finished off in the same way. An alternative to an embroidered border along the edges is to have a facing of a contrasting colour—the facing to come on to the right side of the fabric in this case. Perhaps it could be scalloped or have a zig-zag edge and even then be decorated with some embroidery. The rings for hanging must be placed one at each end and one at each pocket division. They are made by covering curtain-rings with a close buttonhole stitch worked with embroidery thread. They can be worked in each of the colours you have used. Or instead, if you prefer, you could make loops of material and sew them on. The second row of pockets in the illustration is fastened to the first row by fishbone stitch. Additional pockets may be added below, or even single pockets can be made—it all depends on what they are to hold.

Blotter (65)

You will need cotton material and card to make the blotter. For the blotter in the diagram measure a *double* piece of fabric 21½″ by 10½″. This allows ½″ for turnings. Draw out your design and transfer it carefully on to the fabric. The blotter in the diagram has two borders of stitchery with a large star motif on the front and a small one on the back. Try working lemon and white stitching on a navy background or rust and blue on a grey background. When you have completed the embroidery fold the fabric in half on the wrong side and machine along both ends. Clip the corners and turn on to the right side. Fold in the turning along the top edge, but do not stitch it. Mark the position of the central hinge and the pocket and machine down these three lines, fastening off very neatly. Make the two holders for the pad from two strips of material each 9″ by 2″. Fold each of these in half lengthwise and machine along them. Turn them on to the right side, fold in the ends and seam them neatly. These bands can be embroidered to correspond with the borders on the outside if you wish. If you do this, work them before they are machined, and the back of the embroidery will then be enclosed inside the band. Neatly stitch the bands

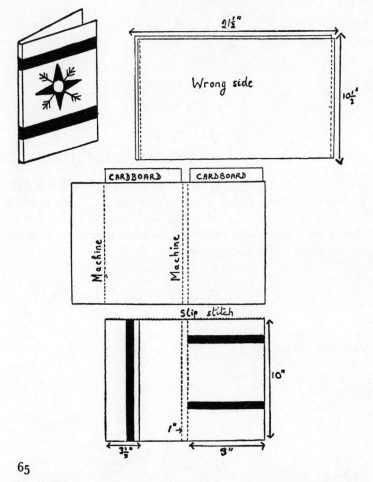

65

into position. Then cut two pieces of very firm card and slip
them down through the top opening. These must fit tightly
and the fabric must be taut. Slip stitch along the top edge.
Lastly fold over the pocket piece to the inside and slip stitch it
to the back at the top and bottom. If a wider pocket is needed,
a hinge can be made at the side like the one in the middle
and small gussets added at top and bottom. When the cover is
to be washed loosen the slip stitching and remove the card. It
can be easily put back and the ends stitched up again.

MORE COMPLICATED STITCHES

IN this second section we come to stitches which are a little more complicated than those of Section I. They can still be executed by the beginner, but with the addition of these stitches her scope is widened, and even more interest and variety can be given to her embroidery.

Stem stitch (66)

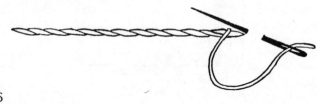

66

This is similar to a back stitch. Bring the needle through from the back and insert it farther along the line, bringing it out half-way back between the second and first holes. Continue in this way, bringing the needle out of the same hole as you used in the previous stitch. Keep the thread to the right of the needle at all times.

Alternating stem stitch (67)

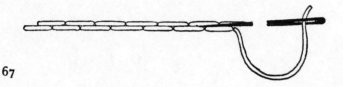

67

This is worked in exactly the same fashion as ordinary stem stitch, except that the thread is for one stitch to the right of the needle and for the next to the left. This is continued alternately, so that the stitches appear like the bricks on a wall. Always use the holes of the previous stitch when bringing the needle out.

French knot (68)

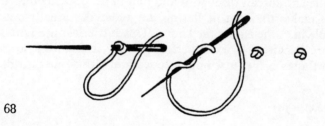

68

This stitch is extremely useful for filling, but needs some care to make a nice round knot. Bring the needle and thread through from the back and hold the thread down with the left thumb. Twist the needle twice or three times round this thread, and then insert the needle very near to where you brought it out. Slide the knot up to the fabric and pull the needle through. The thread must be kept taut all the time, or a loose knot will be the result instead of a firm round one. Some practice is necessary before this stitch can be worked well.

Bullion knot (69)

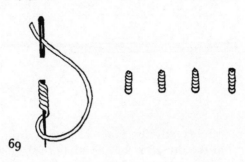

69

This stitch makes a long knot, unlike the French knot, which is round: Bring the needle through from the back and then take a vertical stitch, bringing the needle point out in the same place as you did at first. While the needle is still in the fabric, twist the thread round the end as many times as you need; it depends on the length of the knot, but six or seven will usually be right. Then, holding the twisted thread, carefully draw the needle and thread through it and pull in the opposite direction. This makes the knot lie flat on the material. Finally put the needle in at the end of the knot. This stitch does need practice before it can be worked perfectly. Try it first with a thick, firm thread before attempting to work it with a fine thread.

Fishbone (70)

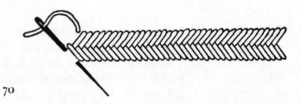

70

This stitch can be used as a filling or as a joining stitch, and it can be worked closed or open. Bring the needle out at the left side and insert it sloping down just past the centre line, bringing it out on the right side directly opposite where you put it in on

the first side. Continue in this way, taking care to put the
needle into the material in the centre just past the end of the
last stitch. This gives the plaited effect down the middle.

Herring-bone (71)

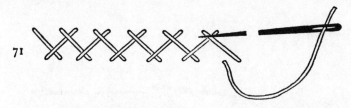

71

This is best worked between two lines. Bring the needle out
on the top line and then slightly farther along on the bottom
line take up a piece of material. The needle points from right
to left. Repeat this on the top line, and so on. The line of
work is from left to right. The regular and even spacing of the
stitches is important.

Threaded herring-bone (72)

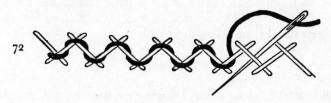

72

Make a line of herring-bone stitch as described above and
then with a contrasting thread weave the needle up and down,
going under the long, sloping stitch and over the point where
the herring-bone crosses.

Closed herring-bone (73)
The same method is used for this stitch as is used for ordinary
herring-bone, except that the needle comes out of the same holes
as those used for the previous stitch. The wrong side should
show a double row of back stitch.

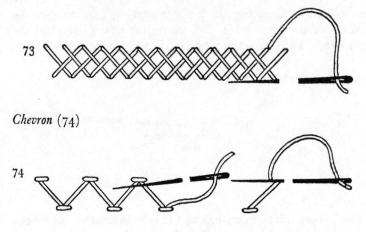

Chevron (74)

This stitch is worked on a double line, as is herring-bone.
Bring the needle out at the bottom line and then take a stitch a
little farther along on the top line, the needle pointing from
right to left.   Draw the thread through, go back a little way to
the right and make another stitch in the same direction, so that
the needle comes out of the hole where it entered the material
before, this being the centre of the stitch. Keep the thread
above the needle. Repeat this on the bottom line, but this
time keep the thread below the needle.

Single feather stitch (75)

This is worked along a line, bringing the needle through from
the back and making a sloping stitch a little farther down.
Hold the thread down with the thumb while making the stitch,
and keep the thread under the needle. The stitch can be
worked on either side, but it is much easier when the arm of the
stitch points to the right.

Feather stitch (76)

This stitch is made in the same way as that in single feather
stitch, with the needle making a sloping stitch towards the
centre, but it is worked first on the right-hand side of the centre

line and then on the left, alternately.   Always keep the thread
under the needle.

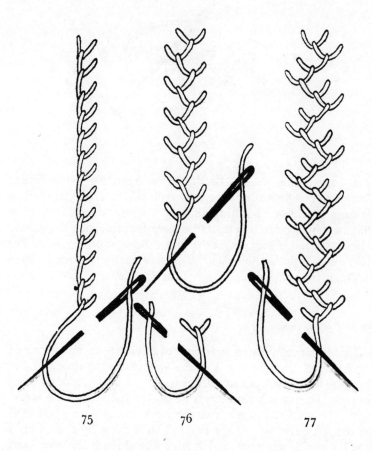

75   76   77

Double feather stitch (77)

   This is worked in the same manner as ordinary feather stitch,
but two or three stitches are made to each side instead of just
one.   The result is a zig-zag line.   Do not forget to make the
stitch a sloping one each time pointing towards the centre, and
keep the thread under the needle.

Chained feather stitch (78)

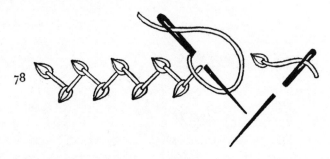

A double line should be drawn to keep this stitch even. Bring the needle out on one side and make a chain stitch in a slanting direction, pointing slightly towards the centre, then make a slanting stitch in the same direction, inserting the needle when it is almost at the opposite line. Bring it out again on the line, but a little farther back. It is now ready to work a chain stitch on the other side. Repeat this from side to side.

Crested chain (79)

This is a complicated variation of chain stitch but is one of the prettiest stitches there is, and is well worth the time spent in learning it. Try it out in thick thread on a fairly loosely woven fabric. The knot must always lie on the left side of the work. Bring the needle through from the back and make a coral knot on the left-hand side of the line. This is done by taking up a small piece of material and having the thread first over and then under the needle. Next slip the needle straight underneath the slanting stitch which has been made, and then make a fairly large chain stitch along the line. Continue in this way— a coral knot to the side, slip the needle under the stitch made and then a chain stitch into the previous one along the line. This stitch sounds more difficult than it actually is. It does look very nice worked on a curved line with the knots on the outside.

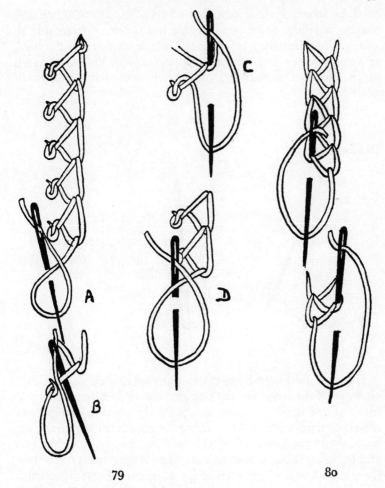

79   80

Double chain (80)

This stitch can be worked along a line or used as a filling for fairly narrow spaces; it becomes ugly when worked on a wide line. First make a chain stitch, then put the needle in at the first hole and work another chain slightly more open and to one side. Then put the needle in the base of the first chain and work a stitch down the line in the usual way. Work the next stitch by inserting the needle in the base of the second stitch and making a chain. Continue in this way working from side to side. When fastening off, take the needle through to the back as you do when finishing off ordinary chain, and then catch down also your second last stitch to prevent it slipping out of position.

Rosette chain (81)

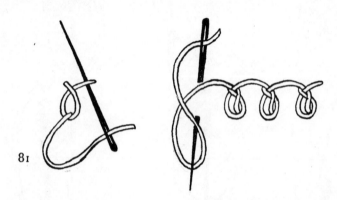

81

This is a most attractive stitch, especially when worked in a circle with the loops on the outside, but it does tend to slip a little. Care must be taken to obtain the correct tension. It is worked from right to left. Bring the needle through from the back, then take a vertical stitch, inserting the needle on the line and bringing it out a little below. The thread must come over the needle first and then under it—as in coral knot. Next slip the needle and thread under the first part of the stitch from below upwards, and then continue from the beginning again.

With the addition of these stitches to those you learned in the first section you can now build up more complex designs. You will find illustrated (82) some ways of using these new stitches just for revision, and then we go on to some fresh motifs.

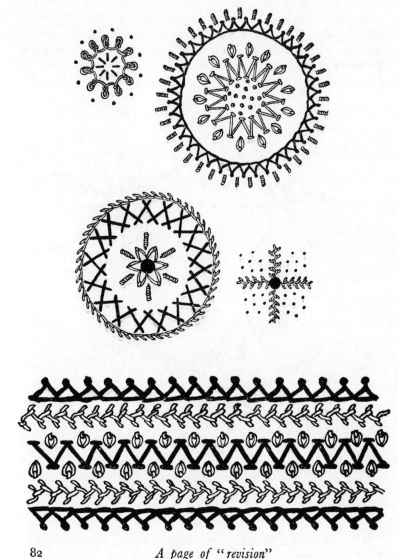

82   *A page of "revision"*

First there is a six-pointed star (83). This is built up from a central spot of chain stitch. Arms of vandyke buttonhole are added and then longer ones of single feather stitch. These are joined with straight lines of buttonhole which form the points of the star. Finally knobs of chain stitch surrounded with single fly stitch are worked in the spaces. Many more variations of the star design can be worked out by the embroideress herself.

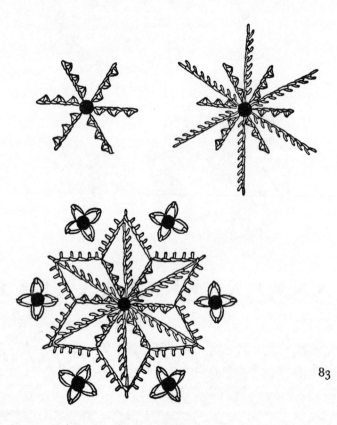

83

We then have a flower design built up on the same lines (84). Each one of these motifs is complete in itself and can be used in an embroidery. Here we have started with a circle of chain, then added single fly stitch and detached chain. After that we

have arms of fly stitch and knobs of chain on the ends. Longer
arms of feather stitch have been worked in between the others
and the edges joined up with a curved line of stem stitch to form
the petals of the flower. Finally an extra outline of crested
chain finishes off the motif.

84

The next illustration (85) shows a more elaborate eight-pointed star. The starting point is the same—a circle of chain stitch. Eight arms of fly stitch are added and then another circle of chain. The points of the star are made with stem stitch along one side and vandyke buttonhole down the other. Knobs of chain are added to the ends of the star points and then branches are worked in the spaces. The central stem is chain stitch and the side branches are fly stitch.

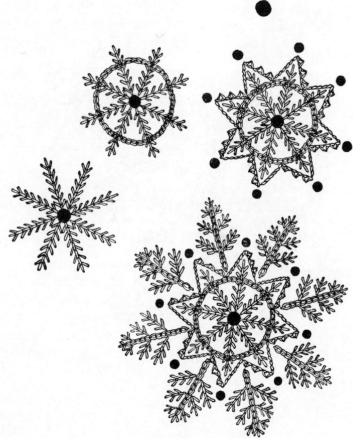

85

Finally, here are some geometrical flower motifs which may be useful when working your designs (86).

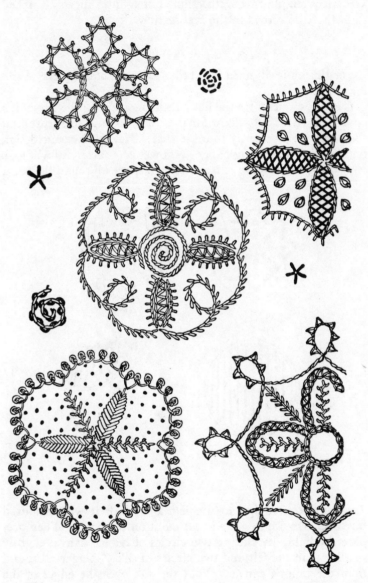

Now here are some instructions for making more articles, using the shapes and motifs that have been illustrated. Again they are fairly simple in construction, but a little more advanced than those described in the first section.

Case for holding a powder compact (87)

For this you will need felt, tailor's canvas and a piece of silk for the lining.

Cut two circles from the felt a little bigger than the size of the compact. This is to allow for the thickness and to ensure that the compact slips easily into the case. Next draw your design on to a circle of tracing paper—a flower or a star motif will look very well—taking care to leave a small space all round the edge.

87

Tack on your design to the felt and work it with coloured threads. Do not forget a small motif on the back. Then prepare the lining by cutting two circles of tailor's canvas slightly smaller than the felt and two circles of silk ½" bigger all round than the tailor's canvas. Fold the silk over the edges of the canvas and tack round, seeing that the silk is quite smooth on the right side. Place each piece of lining on to each piece of felt, wrong sides together, and hem round invisibly. The compact case is now ready to assemble. A good idea is to make an edging of felt by cutting a long strip about ½″ wide, and pinking along one edge. This can be inserted as you stitch the two sides together, and gives a pretty finish. The two sides are joined by a running stitch worked in one of the coloured threads. Join the pieces together for just half-way round the circle, so that sufficient space is left to insert the compact easily, but continue to stitch the felt edging round the edge of the front piece. The running stitch can be whipped or threaded if desired.

Rectangular place mat (88, 89)

To make this you will need a piece of linen 14″ by 11″. The hems are turned on to the right side and are ¾″ wide when finished. Measure off the width allowed for the hems, which is an inch at each side, and draw a thread so that they will be perfectly straight. Next cut a piece of tracing paper the correct size for your design, which will be 10½″ by 7½″. Using your compass, draw on a simple flower shape and work out your stitchery. Use a variety of stitches. This mat was worked in white thread only on blue linen. Next the hems must be turned down and the corners mitred. To do this, cut off the triangular

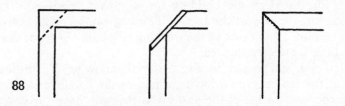

88

corner piece as you see in the diagram, leaving just enough to turn over, so that the fold of this turning just meets the corner. Then turn down the hem in the usual way, and there should be a perfectly straight corner with a line running from the hem to the edge of the mat (88). Slip stitch the folded edges together invisibly. The hem itself in this mat was stitched down with an ordinary running stitch, and a line of single fly stitch was worked just underneath to give a firm and finished-looking edge.

89

Wrist bag (90)

Here is a very simple bag to make. Cut a rectangle 16″ by 12″ and then measure it out according to the diagram. Draw on your flower shape based on a circle and trace it on to the centre of the pattern. You can further enrich the appearance of the bag by adding small pieces of the flower like those that were illustrated in the building up of such a motif—and of course include one for the back. This bag can be made in felt or linen, but I will describe the working of it in the linen, as that is a little more complicated.

Cut your shape out in the material, allowing ½″ turning round the cut edges and having a fold at the handle end, and tack round the edge of the pattern so that you have the exact line on which to stitch later on. Then trace on your design with wax transferring paper, and work out your embroidery. White, lemon and red on a navy-blue background or navy blue, red, white and lemon on a light-blue material are some suggestions. Machine the lower curved edge together on the wrong side on the line of tackings. Press and turn on to the right side. Next cut a piece of tailor's canvas the exact size of the pattern

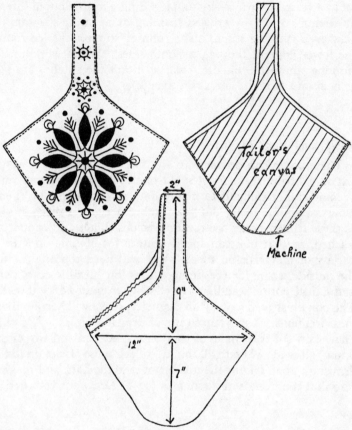

90

and a piece of lining to match, allowing ½″ turning on the
handle edges of the lining.   Place the tailor's canvas over the
lining and tack together, and then machine round the lower
curved edge ¼″ in, with the lining on the inside.   Press and
place inside the outer cover.   Turn in the ½″ turning on the
lining and on the embroidered outside along the handle edges,
folding them along by the edge of the tailor's canvas, and
tack.   You may have to clip the turnings along the curve so
that the material lies perfectly flat.   The seams can be finished

off in a variety of ways—by simple seaming in a coloured thread
or sewing cotton, by crossed seaming or as in the diagram by
very even running stitch.   The running stitch is carried round
the lower edge of the bag on both sides.   When working the
running round the handle make sure that the stitches are just
as neat on the underside as on the upper.

Small round trinket-box (91–6)

These boxes can be made to any size you wish, but I would
advise a beginner to try a small one first, as the bigger ones
become rather difficult to manipulate when assembling them.
Now is the time to try out your embroidery on a piece of silk,
as these trinket-boxes are rather precious things and cannot be
washed, so that one can spend quite a lot of time and use a
variety of materials on them.   You will need some fabric for
the outside, some for the lining, strong but flexible cardboard
and a little cotton wadding as well as your embroidery threads.
The box illustrated was 4½″ in diameter, so we will keep to those
measurements.   Cut your circles of drawing-paper 4½″ in diameter and cut two circles of your outer material and two of the
lining, allowing ½″ extra all round.   Tack these circles on to the
drawing-paper, folding the turning over to the back and making
sure that the front is quite smooth (92).   Draw out your design

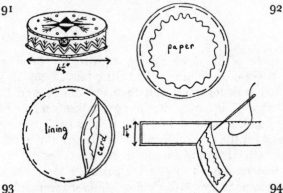

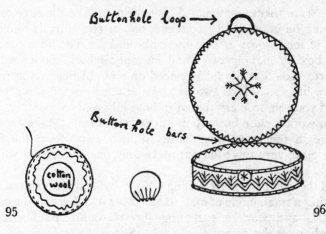

Buttonhole loop →

Buttonhole bars →

cotton wool

95   96

for top and bottom—a star or flower motif will look excellent—
and trace them on to the fabric with transferring paper. Do
not press too much with the pencil, as this work is not washable.
Work your design, going right through the paper if you wish.
Then press it well. Next cut two circles of substantial cardboard slightly smaller in size than the paper ones. Place each
piece of card between an outside and inside piece of material
and seam the edges of these together very neatly with matching
thread (93). The top and the bottom of the box are now com-
plete. The strip round the sides measures $14\frac{3}{4}''$ by $1\frac{1}{4}''$ and is
made in the same way as the top and bottom. Cut two pieces
of drawing-paper the exact length and width and then cover
each one with material, one for the outside, which will be embroidered, and one for the lining (94). The border design can
be very simple—perhaps one of the borders you tried out earlier
on, or perhaps a smaller part of the cover design repeated at
even intervals. The one illustrated has a simple zig-zag.
This could be enriched by using thick and thin stitches on the
up and down lines and the addition of spot motifs or fly-stitch
branches in between. The strip of card must be cut slightly
smaller. Place it between the two lengths of material, having
previously sewn the two short ends of each strip together on the
wrong sides, and seam along the edges neatly. The box is now
ready to assemble. Pin the side strip to the bottom and care-

fully seam them together.   This edge as well as the edge of the
lid can be improved by couching one or two threads round in
one of the colours used in the embroidery.   The lid is fixed to
the box by making two small buttonhole bars about an inch
apart.   See that the lid is placed on straight before you make
these hinges.   Make two or three stitches in the same place
with your embroidery thread to hold lid and box together, and
then work a close buttonhole stitch over them.   Make another
hinge in the same way about an inch away from the first.
These are very tiny; do not make long ones, or the lid will be
slack.

Make the button by rolling a tight ball of cotton-wool and
cutting a small circle of material to cover it.   Turn in the edges
of this and work a gathering thread round, pulling it up
tightly over the cotton-wool (95).   Stitch the back firmly and
work some small piece of stitchery on the front of the button to
correspond with that on the box.   Stitch the button on to the
side exactly opposite the hinges and then make a loop to fasten
it.   Do this by working several threads of embroidery cotton
on to the lid and passing them under the button rather slackly.
Then continue by working a close buttonhole stitch round
these threads.

Flat pad for chair seat (97-101)

These pads can be made to fit any size or shape of chair.
When making your measurements see that the pad will fit comfortably on the chair and not hang over the edges.   Cut your
tracing paper to size and mark on it first the position of the
buttons which keep the padding in place and evenly distributed.   Then build up your design round these circles marked
for the buttons, incorporating them into the design.   The diagram (97) shows a simple star design.   This can be elaborated
by shapes drawn inside the star.   To make the pad you will
need your background material, which can be cotton or wool.
Tack round the shape of the pattern and cut out two identical
pieces, one for each side, so that the pad can be reversed, leaving
$\frac{1}{2}$" turning.   You may decide to have a different colour for one
side.   The one illustrated had red on one side and green on the

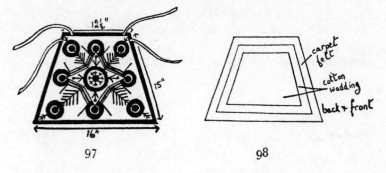

97   98

other with a corresponding change in the embroidery thread
plus black and white. The thread can be thick cotton, wool or
stranded cotton. Trace your design on to each side, using
transferring paper if the material will take it, but tacking on if
necessary. By the way, if you tack on the design, remember to
have two copies of the pattern—one for each side. Work your
design. Next make the inside pad. This consists of a piece of
carpet felt cut to the right size with two smaller layers of cotton
wadding on top and underneath (98). These are tacked together right through to make for easier handling.

Next make a piping to finish off the edge when assembling the
parts. You will need sufficient piping cord to go right round the
pad and a crossway strip of material the same length and about
1½″ wide. Choose a medium thick piping cord and fold the bias
strip round it, securing it by a running stitch just underneath
the cord (99). Turn in the piping at each end and tack.

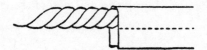

99

Place the piping on the right side of one of the embroidered covers with the raw edges together and the line of running level with the line of tacking round the shape. Tack and then machine this piping on to the cover (100). Neatly seam the

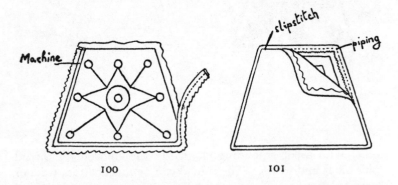

100   101

two ends of the piping together. Turn the piping over so that the raw edges lie on the wrong side, place the felt and wadding on this and then over that place the second half of the cover. Turn in the ½" allowance and hem on to the piping (101). This completes the pad except for the buttons. These can be made by covering wooden moulds with circles of material or by using the metal moulds which can be bought quite easily. On the pad in the diagram the buttons were covered in green material for the red side and in red material for the green side. There was a little embroidery on each one to fit in with the design. When you have finished the buttons stitch them through the pad exactly opposite each other very firmly and pull the thread tight. The tapes for fastening the pad to the back of the chair are made by cutting four straight strips of material 1½" wide and 12" long. Fold these in half lengthwise, turn in the raw edges and seam neatly along. On the end of each one work a tiny motif to correspond with the large design. The tapes can be inserted underneath the pad by loosening a few stitches or stitched in when putting the second half of the cover on.

SIMPLE DESIGNING

Checks, Stripes, Spots, Loops and Scallops

THIS section describes the making of simple designs which involve a little drawing. The easiest way to start, I think, is to choose a material which already has a pattern on it. Using this as a basis for your design, you can soon build up quite elaborate and complicated patterns. For the beginner I would suggest a large checked gingham in simple squares. Start by making circles or stars in different squares, and by varying these and their sequences you will soon obtain some pleasing designs.

Progress from that to drawing zig-zag lines joining the corners of the checks. These can be worked in a variety of stitches—a thin stitch going up the line and a broader one coming down. By making several zig-zag lines with perhaps the addition of some straight ones, and even plus some spots, quite rich and thick designs can be evolved. Diamond shapes with small designs inside them can be made too. Moving on from this, we come to the pleating of checked material. By folding the fabric along the lines of the checks one can obtain quite different effects. For instance, one could fold the material so that the white square is completely blotted out. Several pleats of this kind together give a heavy band, and this in turn could be used for embroidery. The bottom of an apron or a skirt looks very

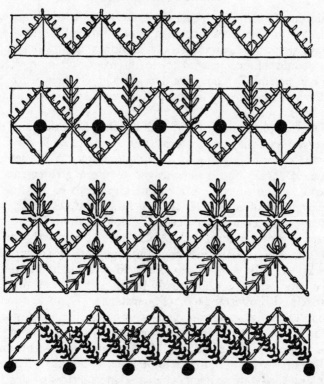

102 (Opposite) *Some designs for checked materials, using embroidery stitches and binding*

103 (Above) *Some further designs for checked materials*

well decorated in this manner. By varying the pleating, all manner of different effects can be made, and it is worth while spending a little time experimenting with checked material. Very charming patterns can be made too from the smaller checks—by making them into stripes with embroidered borders, perhaps emphasising certain lines with thicker thread or blocking out certain squares with stitchery. Again I do urge you to experiment with pieces of gingham, as the variety of decoration is legion. Sometimes the addition of tape or binding can be a help, and of course the straight lines are a great aid to neatness.

Children often find working on these ready-made lines much easier; but this does not mean, of course, that they must always work on such material. Children are rather special and should be encouraged to do the freer and more creative work if possible. They are less critical of their work than adults and more ready to accept funnily shaped creatures and odd lines.

There are innumerable types of checked material, and some have very complicated patterns, but these can be just as useful for this kind of designing as the simpler ones. With the multi-coloured checks one is encouraged to use a greater range of thread and to invent more complex methods of pleating and arrangement of stitch. It is very important, however, when folding or stitching with checked material, to make extremely accurate preparations. The fold must be exactly on the line and the zig-zag lines must go right to the corner of the checks. If this point is not observed one might as well not have the advantage of ready-made lines. A right sense of spacing is important too. For instance, if you are making a border along an apron, you must judge the right position for it. If it is too near the bottom there will be a feeling that it is dropping off the end, and if it is too far up the apron the feeling of a weighty border will be lost; so do take a little time thinking out your spacing when making borders of this kind. Pieces cut on the cross, perhaps containing one whole check, can be stitched on top of the straight material, and these again form a basis for design and decoration.

We now come on to striped fabrics. These, I feel, cannot be used quite so easily as the checked ones. But nevertheless they can be very decorative. Stitches can be worked in between the stripes, and zig-zag or curved lines drawn along them and then worked with embroidery threads just as with the checked fabric; plain tape or crossway stripes can be applied to the background, and simple machine stitching looks very well on striped fabric. In fact, much of the joy of working with this kind of material comes from all the different ways in which it can be joined together. You can see by diagram 104 some of these ways. It is essential, however, that the joins be exact. Even a fraction of an inch out of line will spoil the most carefully planned work.

Remember too that material cut on the cross is inclined to stretch, so that very careful machining is necessary.

104

The third kind of patterned material which is illustrated (105) is the spotted type. This too offers a great deal of scope to the designer. It can be used just as it is and the spots themselves joined up in various ways—with zig-zag, straight or curved lines, or the spots can be used as a basis for circular, diamond-shaped or square motifs, or the fabric can be pleated in a number of ways. By pleating, the pattern of the material is altered so that perhaps the spots come closer together, and these in turn can be made into groups forming spotted stripes. Once again I would like to emphasise the need for extreme accuracy when using this method of pleating to form the basis of your design.   There are some illustrations which show some of the ways in which you can use these patterned materials, but there are many more which you can devise for yourself.

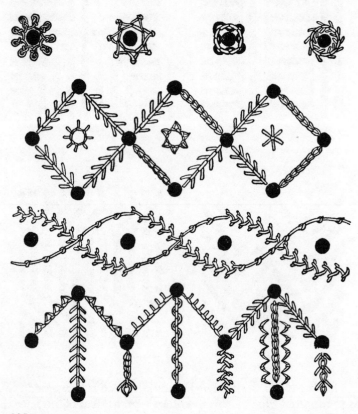

105

From making designs with zig-zag and curved lines on patterned material we can now progress to making simple line patterns with the pencil.   For the moment let us deal exclusively with curved lines, scallops and loops.   To make your scallops, draw round a cotton-reel, a jar or a thimble or any-thing that is suitable in size for your design. Many varieties of scalloped lines can be evolved, by doubling them or intersecting them. Scallops can be extended and made into loops, and these in turn are easily elaborated. Scallops drawn alternately bending in opposite ways may be joined into wavy lines. Some ways of using these curved lines are illustrated here, and some more can be found on pp. 145, 156. Frequently if they are allied with both the straight and the zig-zag lines we have used before they make very pretty designs.

106 *Some ways of using scallops and loops*

Here are some of the things that one can make from spotted, checked and striped materials.

Straight bag

This is the simplest form of bag and has no lining. Cut a piece of material 25″ by 8″ with the fold at the bottom. This allows for all turnings. Draw your design along the spots or checks and work it. The bag in diagram 107 was made of white material with red spots and the embroidery was worked in a matching red thread. Machine up each side on the wrong side and then turn over a deep hem 2″ wide. Stitch this down with running in the embroidery thread and then work a second line ¾″ above the first. This makes the slot for the handles. Undo the seam a little way at each side where you have made the slot and work a buttonhole round the opening, taking care not to catch in any of the underneath material. Make two handles by cutting two 1½″ strips of fabric. Try to cut exactly by the spot, so that when the edges are turned in and the seam machined the handle shows a straight line of spots. Thread each strip right round the slot starting at opposite sides. Turn in the ends of the handles and seam them together.

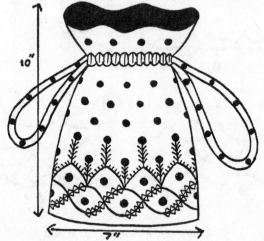

107

Large piece bag

The bag in diagram 108 is made from a 1″ checked black-and-white gingham, with a pleat made about two-thirds of the way down the strip. Cut a piece of material measuring 36″ by 20″, make your pleat and machine along it to hold it firmly. Embroider your motifs; those in the illustration were worked in black and white only. Machine along the sides of the material and make a lining in exactly the same way—some gay colour—red or yellow. Machine these two pieces together along the top edge with right sides together. Cut a circle 5″ in diameter and pleat the bag on to this circle, taking care that the pleats fit in neatly and form a pattern of their own. When cutting the circle for the base make sure that there is a central check.

108

The measurement may vary a little, but the base can be adjusted when you come to pleat on the side pieces. Machine the base to the side pieces on the wrong side. Cut a circle of lining the same size, turn in the edges and slip stitch it inside, covering the raw edges. Make a slot for the cords by either machining or running along one of the check lines about 3″

from the top. Make another line 1″ below this. Make two
buttonholes one at each side of the slot in the same way as for
the straight bag. Couch a white thread along the top edge to
finish off. Section VII of this book gives instructions for making
cords and tassels.

Sewing bag (109)

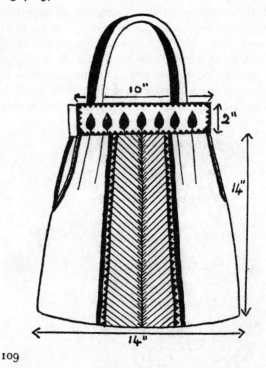

109

To make this you will need some fabric for the outside, a contrasting colour for the inside and two pieces of striped material
cut exactly, on the cross, so that the stripes face different ways.
Join these pieces down the middle and make a V with the
stripes, matching them exactly. Turn in the edges of this strip
and machine it down the middle of one side of the outer fabric
so that it just reaches the fold at the bottom. The measurements for the outer cover are given on the diagram, and the

lining is cut to the same size. Make sure there is a fold at the bottom. When you have put the stripe down the centre, add your embroidery. The bag in the diagram was of navy-blue linen with a navy-and-white stripe and embroidery in thick cotton of red and white. Machine half-way up each side on the wrong side of both lining and outer material. Place lining inside outer cover, turn in side edges of each piece and tack. Make two pleats on each side of centre line facing outwards so that the top edge measures 10″, and tack firmly. Do the same to the lining.

Next cut the pieces which form the straight band along the top. You will need two pieces of outer fabric measuring 12″ by 4″ and two the same size for the lining. There is 1″ turning left all round on this piece, so work your embroidery within this measurement. When this is finished, machine the straight pieces on to the bag, right sides together, and the two lining pieces on to the lining. Next catch together on the inside the two rows of machine stitching—outside and lining. Cut two pieces of firm cardboard 10″ by 2″ ready to stiffen the top, and make the handles by machining together a strip of material with a length of tailor's canvas inside. Place the pieces of card between the outside and the lining, turn in the edges and seam them together neatly, inserting the handles as you go along. It is essential to pull the material very tightly over the card so that it is firm and rigid without any bubbles or puckers in the fabric. This may take some time to do. Lastly finish off the openings at the sides of the bag—those that were tacked earlier on. A running stitch, whipped with a contrasting colour on both the inside and outside, or a simple seaming stitch, will do quite well.

Round bag

This is made in much the same way as the large piece bag, except that the piece of material going round the bag fits the base exactly instead of being pleated. For the sake of clearness the material has been drawn plain, but either checked or spotted materials would be suitable. Either could be decorated with binding and borders like those in diagram 110 or with zig-zag lines of stitching.

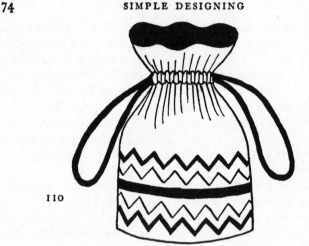

110

Cut a straight piece of material 17″ by 9″ and a circle 6″ in diameter. Embroider the long piece first, and then cut the pieces for the lining exactly the same size. Join the lining and the outside along the top edge by machining them together on the wrong side. Open these pieces out and fold the opposite way, taking care to match the seam. Join again the whole way down the side of lining and outside by machining on the wrong side once more. Here it is necessary to see that binding and embroidery do match exactly on the right side. Turn this piece on to the right side, this time with the lining inside, and tack both pieces together along the bottom edge. Then tack and machine this on the wrong side to the circle cut for the base. Next slip stitch the circle of lining fabric on to the base, turning under ½″ right round and covering up the raw edges. The slot for the cords is made in the way described for the piece bag and straight bag. For a firm base, if one is needed, see opposite (oval bag).

Oval bag

The oval bag in diagram 111 was made in alternate strips of black and white, and each one was embroidered in the contrasting colour. You will see that the design has been made from loops and scallops. These can be enriched by using many stitches. The lining was a soft yellow which looked well with the black and white.

111

Cut three black and three white strips, each measuring 10"
by 4½" (which includes turnings) and join them together by
machine stitching on the wrong side, leaving a ½" turning.
After the embroidery has been completed the bag is made up
in the same way as the round Dorothy bag. The oval base
measures 8" by 4", but when cutting your material allow ½" extra
all round. Sometimes a firm base is required in the bag. If
this is so, cut a piece of card to the correct shape and cover it
with the lining material, seaming round the edges. This can
be taken out when the bag needs to be washed.

Covered coat-hanger and cover, with pockets

A plain wooden coat-hanger is used for the base of the padded
one. Draw round the hanger, leaving ½" extra all round. Cut
this out twice in felt. Draw out your design on a piece of tracing paper—the one in diagram 112 has a pattern of loops and
lines—and tack it on to the felt. After you have worked the
design in gay colours—perhaps red, dark turquoise and lemon
on a black background or red, black and yellow on a grey
ground—pad the wooden hanger. To do this wind a strip of
cotton wadding round and round the hanger, securing it with
a length of cotton (112a). Then seam the two sides of felt over
this, making sure that it is a tight and firm fit. Finish off the
seam by couching two or three thick threads round the edge
(112c).

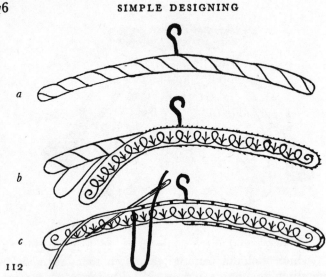

a

b

c

112

The shoulder cover can be made from any washable fabric.
The measurements are given in diagram 113 and the gusset is
two straight pieces each measuring half the length by 2".
Remember to leave ½" turnings on all the edges. The design
matches that on the coat-hanger and can be transferred to the
material with transferring paper. The cover often looks pretty
in a contrasting colour to the hanger—for instance, a yellow
cover with the grey hanger and a turquoise cover with the black
hanger. Work the design before assembling the pieces, not forgetting the small motif on the gusset. Turn under all the hems
—at each end of the gusset pieces and along the top edges of

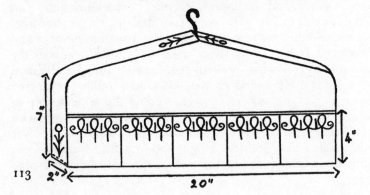

113

the pockets. These can be fastened down with an embroidery stitch. When all the embroidery has been worked, turn up the pockets and machine down the dividing lines. Then tack in the gusset on the wrong side and machine it to the sides. Trim the seam and finally neaten it with bias binding, running it along one side of the seam and then turning it over and hemming it on to the other side.

Apron

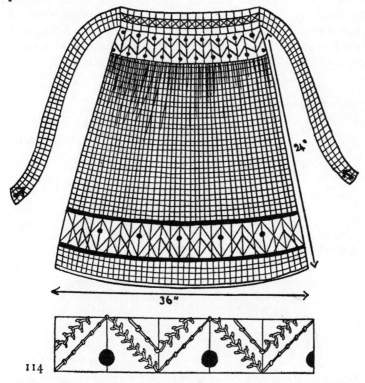

114

The apron is made from gingham, using the full 36" for the width. The length depends on individual taste, but the one in diagram 114 was 24" long without the band. Extra was allowed for the hem and for pleating the checks parallel with the hem four or five times as a basis for the embroidered border. The pleats are first tacked down and then machined, and the embroidery is worked by the check. The hems on the bottom and two sides are hemmed down on to the wrong side by hand. If you prefer it, an embroidery stitch could be used for this. The top of the apron is then pleated, also by the check; these pleats hang vertically as in an ordinary skirt, and are tacked down for about 4″. The embroidered zig-zag lines are then worked. The band is cut to the length required for the top of the apron, with turnings allowed on each end, and an embroidered border worked to correspond with the rest of the stitchery. Machine the band on to the top of the apron, right sides together, and then turn it over to the other side and hem it. Finally, cut two strips for the ties, hem them and insert them between the edges of the waistband. These ties also have a tiny piece of embroidery on the ends as a final touch.

Child's pinafore (115)

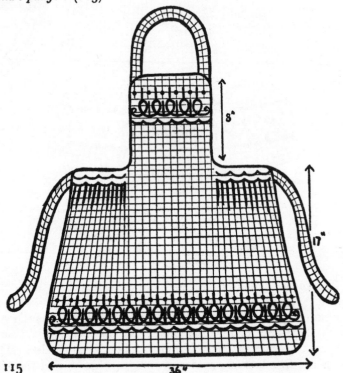

115

This apron also uses the full width of 36″ wide gingham. A smallish check of about ¼″ is best, as the larger ones are not in keeping with the size of the garment.   The full finished length is 25″, but remember when cutting to make both the bib and the skirt a few inches longer to allow for the pleating of the checks. These are pleated downwards and then tacked very firmly. The embroidery design is drawn on to the material and then worked in simple stitchery.   Chain stitch and feather stitch worked in red, white and black on blue and white gingham were the stitches used on the apron in the diagram.   The sides are pleated across and tacked down firmly for 2″, matching the checks.   These side pieces can be worked too if you so desire. All the corners are rounded so that there are no awkward turns to negotiate with the binding.   White bias binding finishes off the apron.   The neck strap and ties are all bound with white and finally hemmed neatly into place.

116   *A suggestion for embroidering the pinafore*

SECTION IV

FILLING STITCHES

BEFORE we move on to further designing with shapes as well as lines it would be useful to know several more stitches. In the main these stitches are for filling shapes. Again they are just some of the many one can choose from, but they are stitches which are quite firm and are no bother to launder or iron.

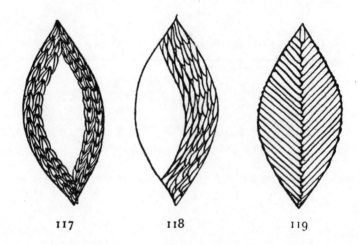

117   118   119

Many fillings of course can be made from the line stitches which are indicated in previous sections of the book. For instance, chain stitch (117) can make a firm, solid filling either worked in lines or round and round without any spaces between the lines. This in its turn can be decorated with single fly stitches worked at intervals on top of it—although in the main it is not desirable to work one stitch over another. Stem stitch (118) or alternating stem also make solid fillings when worked closely together. Fishbone stitch (119) is useful for making solid fillings—especially for leaf shapes, as it can be graduated to fit the outline of the leaf. And then a lighter effect can be obtained by working the stitch with a space in between.

Roumanian stitch also can be worked closed or open, and makes quite an attractive filling. It is worked by having the space divided into three imaginary sections—in fact it is a good idea to draw two lines down the space to be filled. Bring the needle through from the back on the lower edge, then put it into the material exactly opposite on the upper edge, coming out again a short distance towards the centre with the thread below the needle. The needle then enters the material on the right side of this stitch—that is, on the second imaginary line, thus tying down the long stitch. These tying down stitches must be kept even, and if the stitch is very long it can be tied down several times (120).

Herring-bone (121), which is another line stitch, is used for filling too. Both the closed and open type or threaded herring-bone can be graduated to fit various shapes. Several lines worked close together and then threaded look well too.

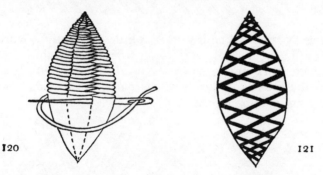

120   121

Other thinner line stitches which are not illustrated as fillings can also be used. Coral knot worked at intervals is attractive. The knots can be fitted in to form a pattern, and other stitches, such as French knot, detached chain or fly stitch, can be worked in the spaces between. This method of using two or even three stitches combined together to form fillings offers infinite variety and scope to the needlewoman. (Diagram 219, p. 158, is an example.) Whipped chain stitch too is sometimes worked solidly or in combination with another stitch. In fact almost any of the stitches which have been illustrated previously can form the basis for a filling. Again I urge the embroideress to experiment with these stitches and make up her own interesting combinations of stitches. There are illustrated below some other broader types of line stitches which, used in regular rows, make interesting fillings. The working must be very regular or they will lose their effect. Continuous fly stitches can be worked in rows side by side (122), or again with the arms of the second row occupying the spaces between those of the first row.

122

Single fly-stitch filling is worked a little differently. Work one row as in the normal way, that is from left to right, and then turn the work upside down and work the second row, seeing that the little tying down stitch comes side by side with the tying down stitch on the first row (123).

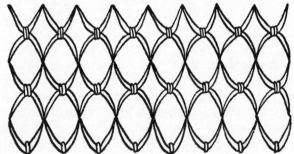

123

Chevron too can be worked in even rows to form diamonds (124) or to make a zig-zag effect, depending on how you space the stitches.

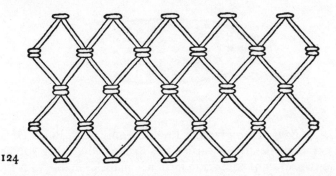

124

There are a number of stitches which give a spotted effect— mainly those which are worked singly. Some of these are illustrated. French knots make a very pretty filling. If they are worked with spaces in between, see that the spacing is regular. A purely haphazard filling does not look so attractive. Worked very closely without any spaces at all, French knots give a rich and solid effect. Then detached chain can be worked in the same way, giving a solid or more open appearance to the work depending on the spaces between the stitches. Again see that they are worked regularly in line with the shape to be filled (125-6).

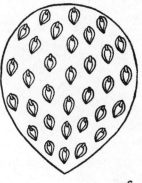

125   126

Cross stitch (127), I think, speaks for itself. This is worked by the thread of the material, and very pretty effects are obtained by varying the sequence of the crosses and spaces.

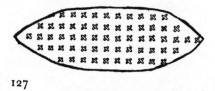

127

Tête de Bœuf or, to give the English equivalent, Bull's Head, has not been described earlier on, as have the other stitches. Make two straight stitches to form a **V** shape as in diagram 128, and then work a detached chain between them. A similar stitch is *Detached Wheatear* (129). This is worked as described for chain and fly. Bring the needle through from the back and then insert it again a little farther along, making a sloping stitch; then work a chain stitch pointing downwards from the middle of the **V** stitch.

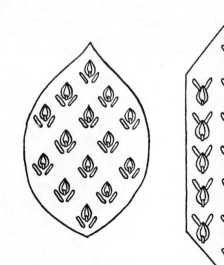

128   129

We now come on to slightly more complicated filling stitches. The spacing again needs to be extremely accurate, or they lose much of their beauty. I think the simplest is *buttonhole* (130). This consists of rows of simple buttonhole worked one under the other, with the upright stitch piercing the space in the previous row. This stitch is sometimes worked without actually piercing the material, but this method is much more difficult to keep even. The buttonhole spacing may be varied, or even the vandyked variety can be worked in this way.

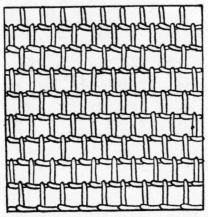

130

Backstitch trellis (131) consists of rows of even backstitches worked so that the stitches meet at the point of piercing the

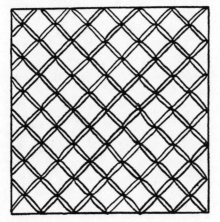

131

material. Extra fillings, such as French knots or detached
chain, are frequently added to the diamond-shaped spaces
made with the backstitch.

Couched filling (132) is made by working one set of threads from

132

side to side crossing over the space to be filled, and then another
set worked in the opposite way. The loose threads are tied
down where they cross by tiny cross stitches or simple tent
stitches. (Tent stitch is a simple diagonal stitch like the first
half of a cross stitch. Care must be taken to see that all the
stitches point in the same direction.) Again the spaces are
often used for further filling if necessary.

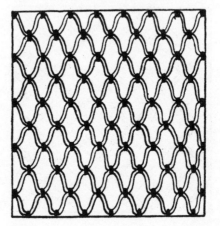

133

Cloud filling (133) is one of the interlacing stitches. The basis
is made by working rows of small straight stitches with the
second row alternating with the first, and then threading these
up and down with a contrasting colour.

The last filling stitch I wish to mention, *Twisted lattice* (134),
is slightly more complicated, but can be worked quite easily
with a little care. The first threads are laid across the space as
for couched filling, but the second set, which are laid the opposite way, must interlace with the first. That is under the first
and over the second and so on, as in very open darning. The
next thread, of a contrasting colour, is interlaced over this
foundation, as can be seen in the diagram.

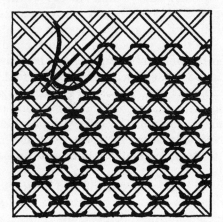

134

DESIGNING WITH CUT PAPER

Having discussed various suitable line and filling stitches, making borders and simple motifs which more or less emanate from the shape of the stitches themselves, and having talked about making designs on materials that already have a basic pattern on them, we now come to making different kinds of solid shapes in which filling stitches and patterns can be used. Even if you cannot draw with a pencil you will find the cutting of paper shapes is quite easy. This is a good training in the selection of sound, firm shapes and the assembling of these gives confidence in planning an effective design. Once you have cut your shapes you can experiment with different arrangements, moving the pieces about until you find a satisfactory design.

From the very beginning you will find it necessary to keep to simple shapes which are not over-elaborated and crowded with small and niggling cutting. This is important, as much of your design can be built up within the cut shape when you come to use your embroidery stitches. A simple and uncomplicated shape can offer unlimited scope for the use of stitchery, and many and varied effects can be obtained, whereas a shape which is over-elaborate to begin with often severely limits the use of stitches and makes in the end for something dull and lifeless. The paper cutting is much the same as that we all did as children, with perhaps a little more attention to the shape of the cuts. Ordinary newspaper will do very well for a beginning. Start by folding long strips into halves, quarters, eighths and so on and then cutting firmly along the top. This will give you a decorative edge, and to go a little farther you can cut

holes of various shapes along the folded edges of the strip.   The
designs one can make with these strips are limitless.   Often the
addition of some lines is necessary to the finished design, but
these can easily be drawn in with pen and ink after the cutting.
There are a few very simple borders illustrated here (135)

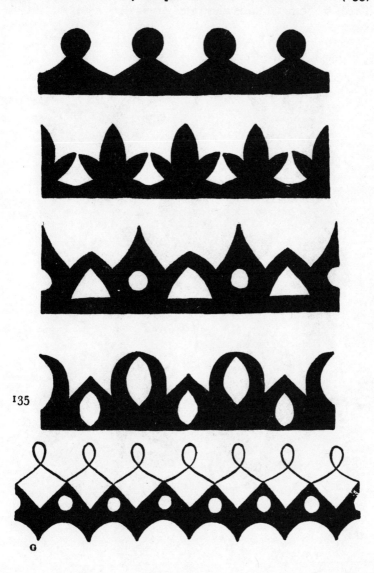

135

Following on from this, the next stage is to fold your paper in half and cut along the open edge to make a single unit, such as a flower or leaf, with the fold in the middle. Again simplicity is important. By folding into four more elaborate flower heads may be cut and even small designs within the main shape. There are some of these illustrated (136–7).

136

137

Leading on from folded paper we can now tackle a freer type of cutting—that is, cutting into the paper immediately without any folding at all. Try this with leaf and flower shapes and you will soon gain confidence and find yourself cutting out quite freely. Try making several shapes, some large, some small and some of medium size, and see if you can build up a complex

flower shape. There is one illustrated (138), and opposite is
shown how it could be worked out in stitchery. With more
shapes again one could assemble a kind of imaginary tree or plant
which when embroidered would make a very pleasing design.
Many shapes taken from nature make the ideal basis for design,
but again one must select the essential points and not endeavour
to make a photographic reproduction of the object. You will
find pictured some butterfly, shell, fish and bird motifs (141–2).
These by themselves would make attractive decorations; for
instance, a flower on top of a trinket-box or some shell motifs
round a beach bag would be quite appropriate. One could

138

make a striped cushion with fish swimming up and down the stripes—each fish based on the same shape but worked with different stitches, so that each had its own individuality. An animal for the top of a cushion would make a pleasing motif, provided that the embroideress remembers she is making an embroidery and not a photograph.

Very often a single cut paper motif is not suitable for the piece of work you are making, and the need for some kind of linking lines is felt. Some very attractive designs can again be built up from a selection of shapes. Keep these down to the minimum, and above all do not have them crowded together.

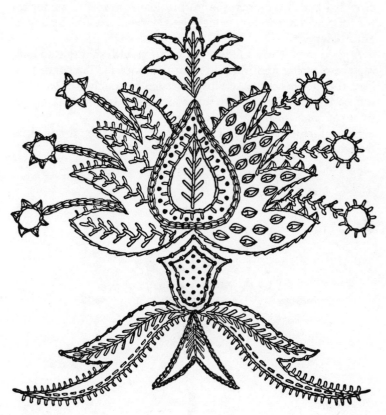

139

When you are satisfied with the arrangement of your design, draw round your shapes on a piece of tracing paper, and after you have made sure that they are spaced well, draw in your connecting lines (140). If you draw these in only one quarter of the paper, the rest of the design may be traced exactly by folding the paper over the quarter that is complete. You can see this method illustrated with a star, a leaf and a circle (144–5) and the bird, leaf and circle (144, 146–8). These are merely suggestions which I hope will stimulate the reader to experiment for herself. Whole pictures and complex designs can be built up with cut paper, and for those who are not confident about drawing it is a good way to start. The clean cutting helps to eliminate crowded and fussy designs, and thus leaves ample scope for the use of various stitches, which is a large part of the joy of embroidery.

A good idea when building up a design with shapes is to have a piece of string and use it to form the loops for the connecting lines that are necessary. This may even be couched down on to the paper and the cut out shapes stuck on before making the final tracing.

Some further ideas for cut paper work may be found illustrated on pp. 97, 100, 158–61.

140

141   *Some cut paper insects*

Cut paper birds, fish and a shell

143 *Cut paper elephant*

144, 145   *Some simple shapes ; and a design based on a star, leaf and circle*

146 *Design using bird and leaf shapes, with the addition of a few lines*

147 *Drawstring bag with shells and anemones :* 148 *design for cushion top with bird, circles and triangles*

SOME SPECIAL TECHNIQUES

*Appliqué, Patchwork, Cross Stitch, Needleweaving, Shadow
Work, Decorative Machining, Quilting, Smocking*

APPLIQUÉ

THERE are some specialised techniques in embroidery, and I
would like to deal with a few of those in more common use.
The first one is appliqué. This, as one can see from its name,
means something applied or stitched on to something else.
Any kind of material may be used, but it is better for the beginner to keep to fabric that is firmly woven and does not easily
fray. Felt is ideal for this type of work, as it is so easy to handle.
It does not lose its shape and can be cut cleanly. Making a
design with cut paper shapes is of course a very good start for
applied work. Here again good shape is essential. The
characteristics of a shape need to be shown, but without fussy
detail. Much detail can be added by stitchery afterwards.

Making an appliqué picture or panel can be quite fascinating,
and one can use a variety of fabrics, bearing in mind the pattern
and texture of the material which often suggests the object
which is being embroidered. A piece of applied work which is
not to have hard wear or which is to be mounted under glass
can be made without turning in the edges of the pieces of
material. A good idea is to cut the shapes in paper first and
arrange them on the background material until a pleasing
arrangement is found.

Once the shapes are cut—and cut quite freely—they may be
assembled on the background material and tacked loosely along
the edges. After this the embroidery is carried out by adding
lines and solid pieces until the picture is complete. Do not

confine the embroidery to lines round the edges of the shapes, but rather let it be part of the picture, linking pieces together and emphasising other parts, so that in the end there is a harmonious whole, and not just a series of isolated shapes outlined with chain stitch.

For an article that is to have wear, this second method of appliqué is better. I think too that if you are not sure of the method of building up with materials you will find this way an easier one. First of all draw out your design on tracing paper, bearing in mind that some of the shapes must be solid ones, and add all the essential lines. Make a copy of this design. In the case of felt tack your design on to your background material. The copy can be used for cutting. Mark out the shapes which are to be applied and cut them out of the tracing paper, and, using these little patterns, cut them out of the felt. These pieces can then be placed in position on the background, using the tacking outline as a guide. Next, hem them down with a matching thread. The work is now ready to be embroidered. This can be done quite freely, some stitching being worked on the applied pieces of felt, as well as on the lines which were included in the design.

This same method may be used for linen appliqué. Make your two designs and transfer one on to the background, using transferring paper. Use the other for cutting out the shapes. As linen is apt to fray, it is necessary to keep the shapes simple and without awkward corners. When cutting out the shapes leave a small turning which is turned under when the piece is hemmed on to the background. These hemming stitches should be almost invisible. When using linen or any material that has a grain, do see that the grain of the applied piece of fabric matches that of the background. When all the pieces are in place the article is ready for embroidery.

Felt pyjama case

This pyjama case can be a very gay piece of embroidery if you use different colours. You will need felt for the outside and silk for the lining. Cut out the felt according to diagram 149

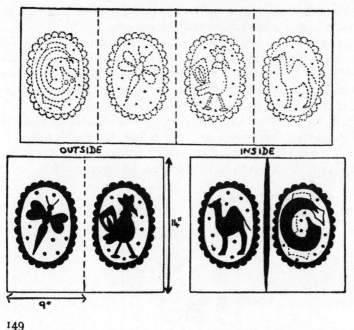

149

and draw out your designs. Those in the diagram were made from cut paper shapes. You will need two copies of each design. Place one set in position on your felt and tack through the lines on to the material. Then tear off the paper, leaving your lines of stitches as a guide. The other designs can be used as patterns for cutting out the felt animal shapes and the felt borders. When you have cut these, place them in position and hem them down invisibly with a matching thread. Then work your embroidery both on the applied shapes and the background. The borders can be enhanced with stars, spots or branches of stitching, and different patterns and textures can be suggested on the animal shapes. Next fold the felt into position and seam it together at the top and bottom with a decorative stitch—whipped running, crossed oversewing or strettle stitch (p. 106). Finally make up the lining to correspond and slip it inside. Finish off the inside opening as you did the top and bottom seams. The lining may be machine quilted. This makes a more substantial pyjama case.

When making this try out an exciting colour scheme. For instance, the outside could be black with white appliqué and the inside white with red appliqué. Perhaps a bright yellow lining on a black-and-white-striped case would make a gay finish. Or each panel could be a different colour—say black, white, grey and red with different coloured shapes applied. If you choose to have more than one colour, the panels should be worked separately and then joined either by fishbone stitch (pp. 42, 106) or machine stitching on the wrong side.

150

PATCHWORK

This ancient craft often appeals to the person who is fond of plain sewing, although embroidery is incorporated into patchwork very often. Extreme accuracy is necessary and a good sense of colour. Patchwork articles vary from those using the tiniest of patches like a pincushion to the largest like a bedspread.

First of all choose a shape for your patch, one that will fit together easily and will eventually make the shape of the finished article. Nearly all patchwork pieces are based on geometrical shapes such as a triangle, square, hexagon, pentagon, etc., all with straight sides so that they will fit accurately together in the

PLATE 3.—*Woollen patchwork bedspread in red, black and white.*
By Winsome Douglass

PLATE 4.—*Black and white wall pockets in felt appliqué. By Winsome Douglass*

final stitching. A template can be cut from tin or very firm thin card and used throughout the work. This ensures that every patch is uniform. If the patches are small, cut the shapes out in paper first and then mount your patch on to this (151). You will need to cut the material a little bigger all round so that it can be turned over the edge of the paper and tacked down. The edges should be perfectly straight, free from pleats and the corners sharp and accurate. Quite elaborate colour schemes may be devised by using different-coloured and patterned materials or by using stripes going in different directions, etc. To achieve the best patchwork a great collection of materials is necessary so that one can choose just the right pieces. By such judicious selection—say of a sprig or a leaf—a new design can be built up within the patchwork. For instance, a selection of patches with a flower motif on them may be inserted to form a circle or a border within the whole piece of patchwork which has a plain background. Sometimes two patches of different sizes are used together, again making an additional pattern in the work.

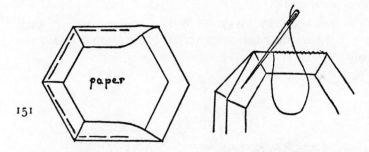

151

The patches are joined as a rule on the wrong side by fine seaming. The tackings are then removed together with the paper. In the case of a bedspread or cushion cover a lining must be added, but in the case of a pincushion or anything that is not to be washed, the paper need not be removed, and no lining is necessary. For the beginner it is a good idea to make the shapes of felt. This eliminates the tacking and turning on to paper. The pieces of felt can be embroidered with appropriate motifs and then stitched together. In this case the stitching may form part of the embroidery and can be worked

H

on the right side—either by simple oversewing in a coloured thread (152) or by fishbone stitch (153), or by crossed oversewing (154), strettle stitch (155), which is inserting the needle twice into the same hole, or faggotting (156).

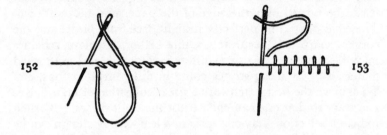

Oversewing (152)

This is simply a seaming stitch, putting the needle through the material at right angles and thus producing a sloping stitch.

Crossed oversewing (154)

This is worked by making a line of oversewing and then travelling back over these stitches using the same holes for the needle.

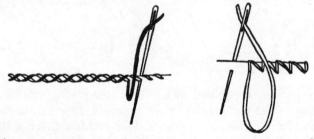

Strettle stitch (155)

Here an oversewing stitch is made, and then the needle is put back through the same hole, making a straight stitch. This is worked along the line, producing first a sloping and then a straight stitch.

Faggotting (156)

Faggotting is best worked when both pieces of material to be joined are tacked on to paper with a small space in between. The faggotting is worked along the space.

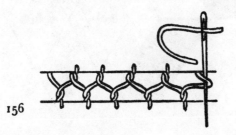

156

The patches need not always be small, and quite large and elaborate objects are made from bigger patches. These need not be mounted on to paper shapes, but even so must be measured with great accuracy. When you have made your design, pin it on to the material and tack round the outside edge so that the tacking stitches make the exact shape of the patch. When stitching the patches together these tackings make a good guide. For cushions, bedspreads, etc., machine stitching is as good a method as any with which to stitch the patches together, and it is less likely to come apart in washing. Faggotting can be used for stitching them together too, but if this method is used the edges of the patches must be finished off with a hem first.

The larger patches give more scope for design. Each patch may have its own individual design and be part of a theme which is carried out over the whole piece of work. The size of each design, however, should be more or less uniform. Sometimes a large overall design may be divided up successfully into a patchwork pattern. For instance, a cushion with a square design could be worked in four patches, perhaps as a counterchange, with white thread on the black patches and black on the white patches. For this type of patchwork, where the design is continuous and not a series of isolated units, great care

157

must be taken to see that the design fits exactly with its neighbouring part, so that there is no break in the line of stitchery (157). For the smaller patches, small embroidered motifs of about the same size can give a jewel-like effect and be very pleasing. On a flat piece of patchwork of this kind connecting lines may be worked to enhance the design.

Some suitable articles for patchwork are a pincushion, ball, chair-pad, cushion, cloth or bedspread. Here is the way to make a:

Felt patchwork ball (158)

This is made from twelve pentagons. Cut out six white ones and six red ones. The cutting must be extremely accurate. Embroider a motif on each section and then stitch them together with an overcasting stitch on the right side in the following way. Stitch five red sections right round the edge of one central white one. Then sew up the sides. Repeat this with the one red section and five white ones. Then fit these two ends together, joining them in the same manner, leaving an opening for stuffing. Stuff very firmly with kapok.

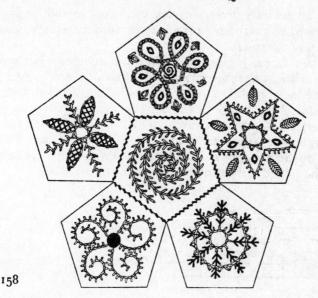

158

CROSS STITCH

Cross stitch is very simple to work, and very rich-looking patterns can be made using this stitch alone. But cross stitch cannot be worked by stamping a transfer on to material, as the whole essence of the stitch is that it is worked by the thread of the material. This is most important. The best way is to plan your design out on squared paper, thinking of groups and solid shapes, and not of individual crosses, or your design will have a thin and scrappy appearance. As well as the spaces to be actually filled in, think of the spaces to be left blank, as these should be pleasing to the eye also. Sometimes the background is worked with cross stitch and the pattern left plain as in Assisi work. As for colour, it is best arranged in definite masses so that the design as a whole has a solid appearance and does not look thin and indeterminate. When working cross-stitch borders, care must be taken with the planning of the corner so that the design has a continuous flow round it. It is essential to work this out on squared paper first.

As for animals, trees, flowers, etc., they should be highly formalised so that they are in keeping with the square characteristics of the stitch.

I would advise beginners to choose a fairly coarse but evenly woven fabric so that the threads can be counted easily. As you become more proficient, finer materials may be used, but the embroidery must still be worked by the thread. The embroidery thread should be smooth and firm so that the crosses are regular in appearance, and not so thin that they do not cover up the background nor so thick that the crosses are lumpy and the thread difficult to pull through the material.

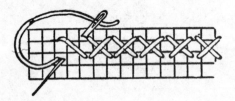

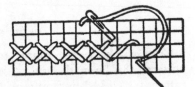

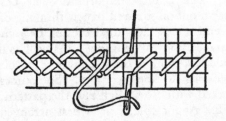

159

The actual making of the cross may vary, but to obtain an even and regular appearance each cross must be worked in the same way with the same stitch uppermost each time (159). It can be worked from left to right, or right to left. Sometimes each cross is worked separately and sometimes, especially for filling large spaces, one stitch is worked along the line and then the cross completed on the return journey.

This stitch is used a great deal in tapestry work, but very often the embroideress endeavours to make too realistic a picture. Try working out your own design. A good idea is to start from the middle and build it up as you work outwards so that your design fits the shape you are working.

I have stressed the importance of working by the thread, but quite lovely designs can be made by using cross stitch on checked material. Here one must use the white squares only, and with a darker thread, very often the colour of the material itself, fill them in with regular cross stitches (160). The same rules of stitching apply to this method as to the working on plain material. The crosses must fit the squares exactly. Very rich and delightful designs may be built up in this way. Once again it is important to use a thread thick enough to cover the square, or much of the beauty of the design will be lost and you will have a thin and scrappy look to your work. In the main a small checked material is most appropriate for this work.

NEEDLEWEAVING

As needleweaving is worked with a needle on already existing material, it comes under the heading of embroidery. It gives scope in the use of broad masses of colour and can be used in conjunction with other embroidery stitches. In spite of the threads being drawn out, it actually strengthens the material in the end.

A fairly coarse material is most suitable for the beginner; one in which the threads are evenly woven and can be removed easily. Choose an embroidery thread which is relative to the thickness of the thread of the fabric and which has some resemblance to the surface of the material. This gives a feeling of harmony as the needleweaving becomes actually part of the fabric.

The design is best worked out on squared paper, keeping to fairly solid blocks of colour, and making step-ladder patterns. The reason for this can be seen when we come to the directions for working.

To commence needleweaving draw out a band of threads to the required depth (161a). These can be cut in the middle and each side of the band drawn out and the ends darned in at each end of the space on the wrong side of the material, or the threads can be cut at each end of the band—that is, if it does not stretch the full width of the material. (But it is rather dangerous to cut the threads at each end unless you are highly skilled with the needle. Then the cut edges must be finished off with close buttonholing to prevent fraying.) I advise beginners to keep to a fairly narrow band at first as the broader ones are more difficult to manage. It is advisable to work a wide band in a small circular embroidery frame. Next hemstitch along both sides of the material, making a ladder effect (161b). This simplifies

161a   161b

the actual weaving, although care must be taken with the groups of threads. If they are too large the needleweaving will be ugly and clumsy. To begin the weaving, lay the end of the thread along one of the groups of threads and weave over it. The needle is passed under one group and over the other, as can be seen in the diagram (161c, d), pressing each row down until the ground threads are covered. The tension is important. If it is too tight holes will occur between the blocks of weaving.

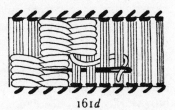

161c   161d

The thread should lie quite easily, and completely cover the background. It is easier to work upwards, turning the work upside down if necessary. To finish off, darn the thread up the back of the weaving.

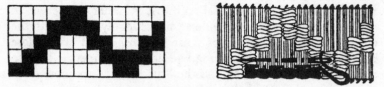

162, 163 *Working out a simple design*

Sometimes a band of needleweaving is carried right round an article and the corners are thus left as open spaces. These can be filled in and incorporated into the design. First of all make a running stitch round the edge and then work over it with close buttonhole to prevent fraying (164–5). Various

164   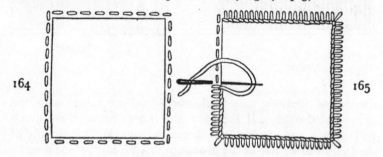   165

methods of filling with bars may be seen in the diagrams (166–9) but these are only suggestions, and will I hope serve as stimulants for further patterns and ideas. In the case of the woven bars, threads are carried across the square, and a second thread is woven under and over them in much the same way as needleweaving. The second method is by overcasting threads which are carried across the square. These again can serve as a basis for a further filling made from a spiral of backstitch round the threads, starting from the centre. Yet another way is to fill small divisions of the square with buttonhole worked as in needlepoint edging (see p. 131).

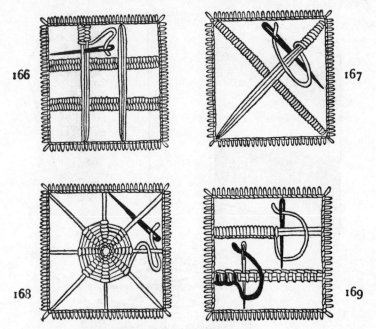

Suitable articles for needleweaving are cushion-covers, stool tops, belts and bands of all kinds, curtaining and even rugs. Very pretty rugs may be made with bands of needleweaving and perhaps some single strands of colour worked in running stitch or woven in in place of a background thread which has been removed. Needleweaving frequently needs some other embroidery stitching to help merge it in with the background so that it is not a completely divorced unit. Sometimes just a row of vandyke buttonhole top and bottom will serve this purpose.

There is illustrated a sewing set comprising pincushion, needle-case and scissors case (170). These perhaps could be allied to a sewing bag having bands of needleweaving as a decoration.

To make the needle-case you will need a piece of material measuring 4″ by 5¼″, and a piece for the lining with the same measurements. These allow ½″ for turnings and ¼″ for the hinge in the middle. Work the piece of needleweaving and make certain that the design fits completely into the space. Then

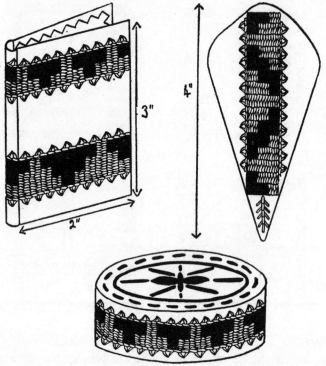

170

turn in all the edges of both lining and outer material and tack them down. Place these two together, with the right side outside, and make two rows of running stitch down the centre with $\frac{1}{4}''$ space between, joining the two together. Next cut two pieces of firm card each measuring $2\frac{3}{4}''$ by $1\frac{3}{4}''$ and insert these between the two layers of material on each side of the hinge and then seam very neatly right round. Cut a piece of felt or flannel with pinking shears and stitch to the inside with whipped running or other appropriate stitch.

To make the scissors case, first draw round your pair of scissors on a piece of stiff paper and cut this out for the pattern. Cut out the two outside pieces, leaving a turning right round, and work the piece of needleweaving down the centre. Mount each piece of lining on to a paper shape by turning the edges over the paper and tacking through. Seam neatly each piece of lining to each piece of outer cover.   Then seam the two pieces together, leaving sufficient space open at the top so that the scissors slip in easily.

SHADOW WORK

This kind of embroidery is worked on transparent material such as organdie or nylon.   Because of the nature of the fabric it is essentially a delicate type of work, and this should be borne in mind when planning the design and choosing the thickness of the thread.   If either of these is too heavy in quality, the work will look ugly, clumsy and out of place.   The shapes of the design are as a rule filled in with double backstitch, which gives the straight stitching on the right side while the crossed stitching or closed herring-bone comes on the wrong side (171). This can be seen faintly through the material.   Hence the name—shadow work.   Stem stitch and other fine line stitches are frequently used on the right side, but nothing heavy or clumsy.   Eyelet holes are sometimes incorporated into designs for shadow work.

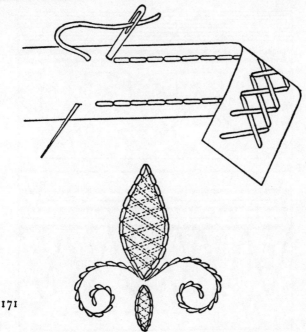

171

DECORATIVE MACHINING

It is necessary to distinguish between decorative machining and machine embroidery. The latter needs special appliances and a great deal of skill. In the former the ordinary household sewing-machine is used, without any special attachments. For those who enjoy using the sewing-machine this type of work has possibilities. As in other embroidery, extreme accuracy is necessary, but for the skilful machinist this should present no problems.

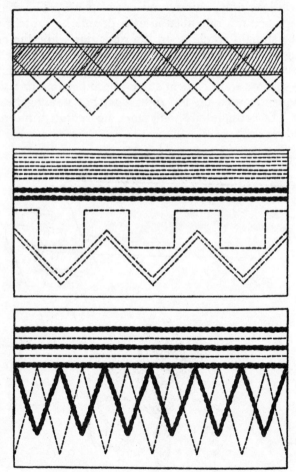

172

The designs are usually made up of straight lines and can often be allied with straight and bias bindings and pleating of the material. Different-coloured threads may be used, and the stitching down of hems and facings with them is an addition to the design. There are some diagrams (172) to illustrate some of the many simple designs which are possible by using the sewing-machine. The design is tacked on to the material and the tackings used as a guide for the machine stitching. Zig-zag lines which are fairly close together should be marked with a dot for each point. When turning a corner, machine up to the dot, and when the machine needle is down, stop the machine, lift the foot and turn the work in the new direction, lower the foot and continue. You will see illustrated in the diagram some rows of thicker machining. This is worked with machine cotton threaded in the machine, and thick embroidery cotton wound on to the bobbin. The machine stitch must be lengthened to its fullest extent and the stitching is worked from the wrong side. One need not stop at straight lines and zig-zags, although it is a good plan to start with them; scallops and other very simple geometrical motifs are suitable for this kind of decoration. One must always bear in mind, however, that the rigidity of the straight line of machine stitching is much of its charm, and not try to force the technique to copy a piece of hand embroidery.

QUILTING

I have included quilting among the embroidery techniques because there are many people who like plain sewing and to whom this craft will have an appeal. It is extremely useful and can be very beautiful. As you may know, it is one of the oldest crafts, and no doubt had its origin in the desire for warmth. Most articles which are quilted today serve that same purpose and we find quilts, hot-water-bottle covers, tea-cosies and bed-jackets being quilted and used for warmth as well as cushions, handkerchief sachets and nightdress-cases which are mainly decorative.

The warmth is derived from the stitching together of several layers of material, the top one for beauty of appearance, the middle for the warmth and the underneath for durability. The

choice of material is important in quilting, as in other types
of embroidery. For the top layer something soft and firmly
woven is best, such as crêpe-de-chine. Most of the old quilting
was worked in soft cotton material. A plain fabric is best, as
the quilting is sufficient decoration in itself. The underneath
lining requires to be strong yet soft, and again a soft cotton is
best. In some articles two lots of quilting are made so that the
lining is a separate piece of quilting, as in the case of a bed-
jacket. The middle layer consists of cotton-wool, flannel or
domette. The more thicknesses put in the middle the greater
the relief of the quilting when it is finished.

The three layers are put together and tacked firmly before
any quilting is started. The tacking is important, as there
should be no movement of the material, and above all no pleats.
The quilting should be quite smooth. Start tacking from the
centre of the piece of work and tack in straight lines towards the
outer edge of the material in a star fashion, smoothing out
the fabric as you go (173). Use a matching sewing silk for
the stitching.

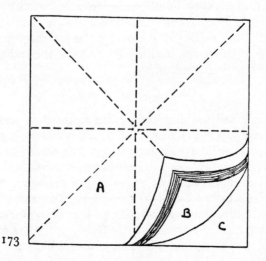

173

The quilting pattern is important. In the old days the Dur-
ham and Welsh quilters used household articles such as a wineglass or a cup to make their designs, or took something from

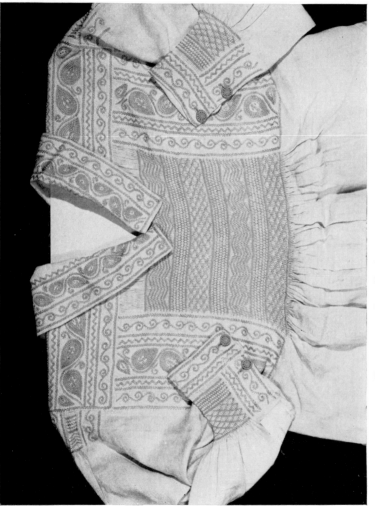

PLATE 5.—*Detail of a smock.   Traditional*

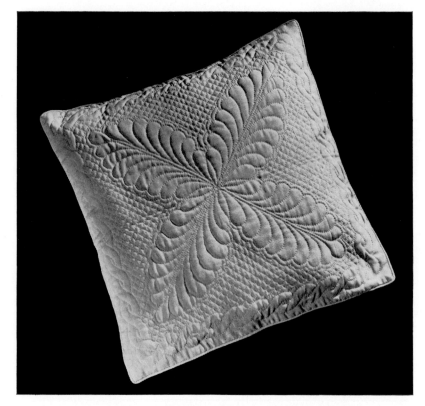

PLATE 6.—*Quilted cushion.   By M. Lough*

nature such as a leaf or a shell and built their design round it (174–7). The design should cover most of the area of

174 *Wineglass*

175 *Shell*

176 *Feather*

177 *Rose*

the article and be evenly distributed so that there are not large patches of unquilted fabric, giving a bumpy effect. Aim at an overall design of light and shade when finished. Much of the charm of quilting lies in this effect of the light catching the relief formed by the pattern. If your pattern is a repeating one, the motif can be cut from stiff paper and placed on the right side of the material. Scratch round the shape with a needle and use this line as a guide. More complicated patterns are best cut up in pieces and the stitching worked round a small piece at a time until the whole design is built up. I think that quilting is best worked from the right side, although some people favour working from the back. If you work from the back the design should be transferred on to the underneath material and the stitching worked over the lines.

The stitches used are usually a running stitch, backstitch or chain stitch. Chain stitch is only suitable for quilting with a thin padding. The more usual is a running stitch which in actual fact is better worked as a stab stitch—that is, one stitch at a time, pushing the needle right through to the back and then bringing it straight up to the front. This makes for much more even work. The quilting should be even on both sides and the stitch pulled rather tightly. The work is better started from the centre, and any possible bubbles of material can be smoothed to the outside as the work progresses.

Some simple and decorative forms of quilting are used in embroidery for tea-cosy linings and pads, such as those in trinket-boxes. For instance, rows of simple running stitch can form quilting—or it is possible to use the running stitch for different designs. All these can be worked in an embroidery thread which perhaps will match up with the main work. Other stitches may be worked, such as chain stitch made into solid circles, or cross stitch, or even straight stitches formed into a star. Care must be taken to arrange such motifs evenly and see that they are equally neat on back and front of the quilting. Try some decorative quilting out on patterned materials. For instance, you could devise a pattern on striped or spotted materials, using the material as a basis for your quilted design.

Quilting can also be done by machine. Very often this type of work is used for linings. As a rule the designs are kept to those built up from straight lines so that the machine is stopped as little as possible. All-over designs of squares or diamonds are most usual, although the design of hollow squares one inside the other, decreasing in size, makes a charming pattern.

SMOCKING

Smocking is another ancient craft, and in bygone days the farm worker always possessed a smock. It was usually made in a simple fashion from rectangular pieces of material. The skirt part was gathered into the yoke and the neck was a square wide enough to slip over the worker's head without any difficulty, and back and front were alike. They were usually made from a strong linen and decorated with smocking where the extra fullness was gathered in—at the yoke and cuffs. As time went on, the yoke itself was embroidered and very often indicated the particular craft of its owner. For instance, a forestry worker might have had a design made from circles representing the cross sections of tree branches. In fact one could tell which part of the county a person came from by the design worked in his smock. As a rule the embroidery was carried out in a matching thread or one slightly darker than the smock itself, and very beautiful it looked.

Today, of course, we use smocking mainly for children's clothes, blouses and aprons and also use gay colours, which add very often to the decorative quality of the smocking.

Most materials can be smocked, but a beginner should start by using a firmly woven cotton or a fabric that will pleat easily and stay firm while the smocking is being worked. The thickness of the embroidery thread again depends on the weave and quality of the material.

The amount of material necessary varies according to the fullness required, but as a rule it is best to allow three times the amount required by the finished width.

Even smocking depends largely on the regularity of the tacking and pleating, so it is wise to spend some time on this in order to achieve a good result. Some materials lend themselves well to the tacking, such as checks and spots. If they are printed quite evenly one can pick up each spot or alternate spots, or tack along the lines of the checks, perhaps picking up all the dark squares or light ones as you wish. Very pleasing effects of light and shade are obtained when smocking checked materials, if some thought is given to the method of tacking.

For a plain material one can rule a line of dots, taking care to space them evenly, and then pick up one third of the space between them; a much easier method is to buy a smocking dot transfer. These are available in different sizes and are stamped on to the wrong side of the material with a hot iron. Care must be taken to keep the dots in line with the thread of the fabric. In this case, when tacking, pick up each dot, taking care to pick up the same amount of material each time in order

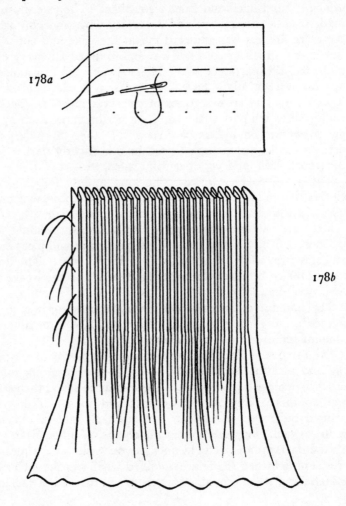

to ensure even pleating. The tacking thread should be long enough to stretch along the whole width of the fabric. Start with a knot and a double stitch to make sure the thread does not slip, and after tacking along the line leave the loose thread hanging. When all the rows have been tacked, pull up all the threads together, so that the pleating is the required size. The smocking does give a little when the tacking threads are removed. Knot the threads in twos down the side so that they will not slip and the work will be ready for the embroidery (178a, b).

There are many designs which can be devised by using the different smocking stitches, and it is wise to work out your pattern first, so that if you are going to have diamonds or zig-zags you can calculate exactly the number of pleats you will require. Diamonds and zig-zag lines should start and finish with a complete motif. Bear in mind too that the pleats themselves can form a pattern between the rows of embroidery—opening and closing as you vary the type of stitching. This should form part of the overall design.

Care should be taken as well with the depth of smocking that is worked. The amount of embroidery should be in proportion to the size of the garment. The weight of the colour too is important, as the smocking should appear to be part of the garment and not just an extra piece of decoration.

The actual smocking is worked from left to right. The needle is brought through from the wrong side and the top of each pleat picked up. It is advisable to have sufficient thread in the needle to finish the whole of one row, fastening off on the wrong side again.

There are illustrated some of the more commonly used smocking stitches (p. 126).

Stem stitch (179)

This is worked as the usual embroidery stitch, either keeping the thread always above the needle or always below it.

Alternating stem stitch (180)

This forms a brick pattern and is worked in the same way as ordinary stem stitch with the thread placed alternately above

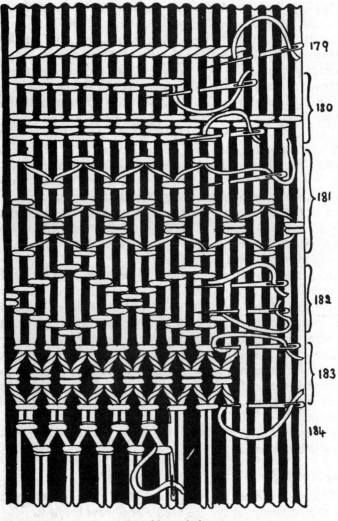

179–184   *Smocking stitches*

and below the stitch. This stitch is very good for solid bands when worked in close rows, or it can be worked to form solid triangular or diamond shapes. Each of these should be worked separately, the work being turned upside down on alternate rows and the needle picking up one pleat less each time until the apex is reached.

Diamond stitch (181)

Again the stitch is worked from left to right. Bring the needle up through the first pleat, then pick up the second pleat exactly level and with the thread below the needle. Then pick up the third pleat with thread still below the needle, but a quarter or half an inch above the first stitch. Pick up the fourth pleat with thread above the needle and then the fifth pleat level again with the first stitch and thread still above the needle. Then continue as from the first stitch. This is quite easy if you remember to pick up a new pleat with each stitch. The other half of the diamond is made by working a similar row immediately underneath and arranging it so that the top stitch of the second row meets the bottom stitch of the first.

Zig-zag stem stitch (182)

This is another form of stem stitch. Starting at the lower edge of the zig-zag, pick up each pleat, placing the needle a little higher up with each stitch and keeping the thread below the needle until the top of the zig-zag is reached. Then start to come down in the same way, changing the thread round at the top stitch, now working with the thread above the needle. Change it round at the bottom stitch and continue in the same way. This stitch may be worked in rows close together or with spaces between them or to form diamonds. The number of stitches taken to reach the top of the zig-zag determines the size of the diamond.

Chevron (183)

This is worked in much the same way as the ordinary embroidery stitch, and is very similar to diamond stitch. Bring the needle up through the first pleat, then pick up the second pleat

exactly level, with the thread above the needle. Then pick up
the second pleat again a quarter or half an inch lower down
with the thread still above the needle. Pick up the third pleat
again level with the last stitch but with the thread below the
needle. Again pick up the third pleat level with the top stitch
and thread below the needle. Then continue as from the
beginning. Rows of this stitch worked together form diamonds
if the top stitch of the bottom row is level with the bottom stitch
of the previous row.

Honeycomb (184)

This stitch and the last one are the most elastic of the smocking stitches. Again it is worked on a zig-zag principle, like
chevron and diamond stitch. Bring the needle up through the
first pleat and then take a stitch through the second and first
pleats together. Put the needle into the hole made in the
second pleat, forming another stitch over the first one, and
carry the needle down through the back of the second pleat,
bringing it out a quarter or half an inch lower down. Then
make a stitch through the second and third pleats together, put
the needle in the hole in the third pleat and carry it up behind
so that it emerges level with the first stitch. Continue up and
down in this way with the needle going behind each pleat and
making a double stitch on the outside.

Sometimes a piece of smocking is worked at the side of a garment or perhaps does not occupy the full width. In this case a
finishing stitch at the side is often an improvement and rounds
off the piece of smocking. Perhaps a row of vandyke buttonhole, feather stitch, whipped chain or some other embroidery
stitch would make an appropriate finish to the smocking. The
tacking threads are removed when the smocking has been
completed.

FINISHINGS

Hemstitching, Needlepoint, Edges, Cords, Handles, Tassels,
Fringes, Fastenings

VERY often a beautiful piece of embroidery is spoiled because of poor and inappropriate finishing. The hems, seams, fastenings and additional decorations are just as important as the main body of the work, as it is only when all these harmonise that a complete and beautiful embroidery is achieved. All finishings must appear as part of the whole work and not as extra pieces stuck on as an afterthought. Frequently the embroideress must try out different kinds of hems, etc., until she finds the one most suitable for the work. There are some diagrams of the more usual ways of finishing off hems which I hope will be helpful.

HEMS

There are numerous methods of fastening down hems. Of course plain hemming is often useful even in embroidery. Sometimes a facing is necessary. This is frequently a crossway strip of material sewn on to the right side of the work and then the whole piece folded over to the wrong side and hemmed down, so that the seam is at the edge of the material. If the edge is a straight one, then a facing which is cut on the straight of the material is better. An edge is often finished with a bias binding. This too is stitched on the right side and folded over the edge and hemmed on the wrong side along the first line of stitching. This leaves a strip of binding showing on the right side. Sometimes this method of finishing a raw edge is allied with an embroidery stitch worked just inside the edge of the

binding.   A softer outline and a weightier effect along the edge
are achieved in this way.   Instead of turning a hem with plain
sewing, try an embroidery stitch and use this to fasten the hem
down.   All manner of attractive borders may be devised by
using this method.   Sometimes the hem is turned on to the
right side and an embroidery stitch used to fasten it down
there.

We now come on to hemstitching.   There are many designs
in hemstitching, but here we will keep to some simple ones.

Hemstitching (185)

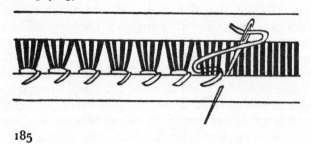

185

First draw out the required number of threads and then turn
down the hem until it is level with the drawn threads, and tack
it.   The hemstitching is worked from left to right and from the
right side.   Bring the needle through the hem from the back
and pick up from right to left three or four threads, and then
insert the needle in the material, taking care to pierce the hem
at the back, just at the right of the bundle of threads.   Then
continue, picking up the next bundle and making a stitch into
the hem at the right of the group of threads.   A second row of
hemstitching may be worked along the other edge.   If the
same group of threads is picked up the stitch is known as
Ladder Stitch (186).   A zig-zag effect known as *Serpentine Stitch*
(187) is obtained by working the first row as for ordinary hemstitch and then working the second side so that the needle picks
up half the threads of one group and half of the next together.
Even numbers of threads should be grouped together for this
variety of hemstitching.

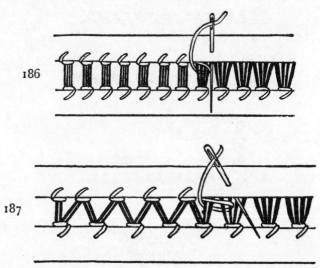

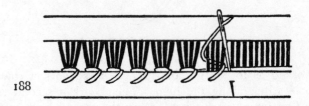

Antique hemstitch (188) is worked from the wrong side and in the same way as ordinary hemstitch except that the needle is

186

187

188

inserted between the hem and the material. In this way only the short stitches which fasten the bundles together appear on the right side.

Sometimes when drawing threads right round a square, a hole is left at each corner. These should be filled in with one of the methods described in Needleweaving. If you wish to avoid a hole, cut your threads which are to be drawn in the middle and draw out each side to the desired place. Then carefully darn the thread in along the back of the material.

Another decorative edge, but one which takes some time to work, is *Needlepoint* (189). It consists of rows of buttonhole

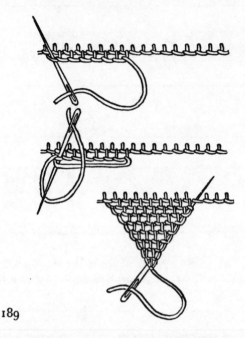

189

stitch worked as for buttonhole filling. First work a row of
buttonhole stitch along the hem. Then work a second row
into the first for seven stitches; carry the thread back to the
beginning, missing out the first stitch, and work a third row into
the previous one and over the thread which you carried back.
This time only five stitches will be necessary. Continue in this
way, missing a stitch at the beginning and the end until only
one is left. Run the needle and thread along the right-hand
edge of the triangle and commence the next one. The size of
the triangles can be adjusted by varying the number of stitches
along the first row.

One final word about hems. Wherever possible the corners
should be mitred, as this gives a neater finish to the embroidery.
This process has been described earlier in the book (p. 55).

On some articles an extra edge is necessary. For instance, a felt tea-cosy looks better when finished off with a felt edge. These can be cut easily from the felt as there is no fear of fraying ends. A pointed or scalloped border looks attractive. Cut the pattern in paper first and then cut round it on the felt. Sometimes embroidery may be added to the felt strip if the piece of work needs it. This type of border need not be confined to felt only. It is often appropriate when made in cotton material. To do this fold your strip of material in half lengthways with the fold to the top. It should be wide enough to allow for a turning both at the top and bottom edges. Mark off your points or scallops on the wrong side with a pencil or tacking stitches and then machine along the lines. Stop the machine at the points with the needle in the material, lift the foot, turn your material, lower the foot and continue with the machining. Then cut round the stitching, leaving a small turning and taking care to cut right down almost to the stitching at the inside points. The material should be cut straight across at the top points. Turn the whole strip to the right side and press well before adding it to your work (190).

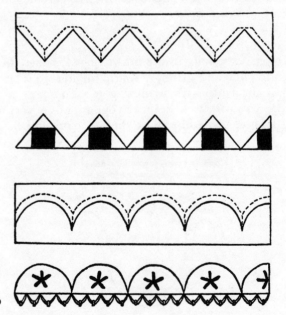

190

When using checked material try experimenting with cross-way strips as facings and bindings. Allied with some embroidery they make very attractive finishings.

Piping is another method of finishing a piece of work. You will need piping cord, which can be bought in a variety of thicknesses, and a crossway strip of material. Fold the strip over the cord and run the two thicknesses together just under the cord, so that it is held quite firmly in its cover. The piping is then ready for insertion between the two layers of material. The piping itself is sometimes embroidered. For instance, groups of satin stitch worked at intervals will give a chequered effect.

Earlier on (p. 75) I have described couching as a method of covering a seam. The number of threads should be varied according to the thickness required, and there are various stitches described in the first section which may be used to tie the threads down. Sometimes couching is not a thick enough covering for a particular edge, and I would then recommend covering the seam with a cord. The correct thickness should be determined with a few strands of cotton before the final cord is made.

CORDS AND HANDLES

Very often, especially in the drawstrings for bags, the cords are much too thin and stringy. A firm round cord is best, so do not skimp the cotton when making it. To make a twisted cord (191) you will need to make your strands of cotton three times as long as you will require the final cord to be. Cut as

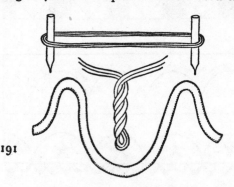

191

many lengths as you need (the more lengths, the thicker the finished cord), and tie them at each end.   Then place a pencil through the loop at each end and twist these in opposite directions, keeping the threads between quite taut.   If the cord is a long one, then two people, each holding one of the pencils, should twist it.   When it is quite tightly twisted, hang a weight from the middle—a pair of scissors will do quite well—and bring the two pencils together; the cord should twist up quite naturally.

The other type of cord—a knotted one—is a little more difficult.   It is worked on the fingers (192).   Tie your two pieces of thread A and B together at one end and hold the knot between the thumb and second finger of the right hand.   Loop A, or the left-hand thread, over the first finger, keeping hold of the end of this thread with the third and fourth fingers.   Then with the left hand insert the forefinger into the loop and bring through the other thread B, holding the end of that with the third and fourth fingers of the left hand.   Now take hold of the knot with the left hand and release the loop held by the right forefinger, pulling the thread tightly.   Repeat these processes,

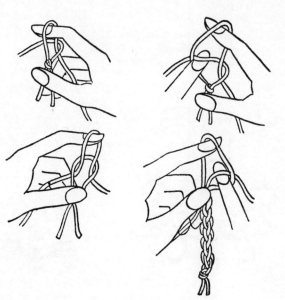

192

changing from left to right hands alternately. A beginner should practise this with thick string until the correct rhythm and tension are obtained.

A stitched piece of material can be used to draw up a bag, instead of a cord. Care must be taken to cut the fabric on the straight and sufficient allowance made for turning in the edges. Tack these firmly and then machine down the two sides. This makes a very firm drawstring. If the stitched string or handle is fairly wide, then it is advisable to put a strip of tailor's canvas between the two layers of material for additional strength. Handles are often inserted in between the outer fabric and lining and invisibly stitched, but if by chance they are stitched to the outside of the bag, let the stitching form part of the design. Sometimes a little embroidery round the end, or even on the end of a handle, keeps the continuity of the design. If machine stitching is used make it fit in with the pattern. Sometimes rows of straight machine stitching, or a cross or a triangle, are used for the stitching of handles (193).

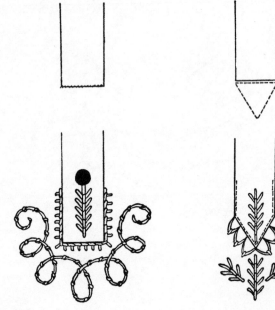

193

There is one handle fastening which should be described in detail—that which is attached by a ring (194). In this case the handle is usually stitched round a piping cord with an inch or two left open at each end. Fold the piece of cord at the end round the ring and stitch it securely back on to the main piece —thus forming a loop with the ring hanging in it. Then take the loose piece of material and fold it round in the same way so that it covers the end and stitch it neatly and firmly on to the main piping. Keep this piece of material opened out and not folded as you had it when covering the piping. Sometimes a piece of tailor's canvas is placed underneath this end piece for additional strength. Make a tab as in the diagram with a fold at the top. This is folded over the bottom half of the ring and the whole tab is stitched on to the bag.

194

Tassels

Cords and drawstrings need their finishing too, and so we come on to tassels (195–6). These of course may be varied enormously but the making of a basic tassel is a good starting point. Once again, let me stress the point of making the tassels quite fat and rich-looking, and not thin and meagre—these will only spoil the look of the whole work. Take a piece of card of

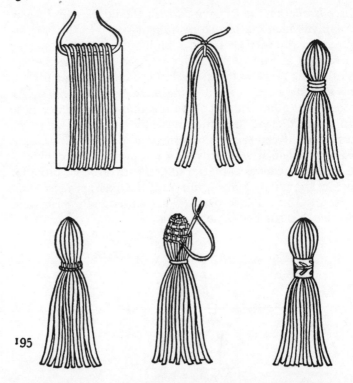

195

the same length as you require the tassel to be and wind your
thread round it. Slip a piece of thread through the loops at the
top and tie this in a double knot. This knot is slipped round
underneath the tassel afterwards. Slip the threads off the card
and cut them at the bottom. The tassel necks can be made in a
variety of ways. The simplest is to bind several threads round
the tassel a little way from the top. A piece of embroidered felt
could be stitched round or buttonhole stitch worked round a
binding thread. Sometimes the whole head of the tassel is
covered with buttonhole stitch. This is started at the top and
rows worked one below the other, each one piercing the stitches
of the previous row as in buttonhole filling.

Very attractive tassels can be made in felt. The piece of
felt is cut into strips which do not reach quite to the top of the
material, with a pair of sharp scissors. The strip is then rolled

up and carefully stitched at the side and centre so that it does
not unwind. Various heads for this type of tassel are illustrated
in diagram 196.

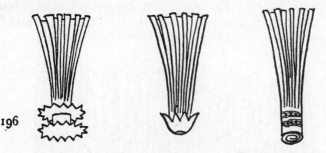

196

The proportion of the tassels is important. Do not make the
head too long or cut the ends too short or even make the neck
too long and thin, or you will have something clumsy and ungainly instead of a beautiful flowing tassel.

Tassels need not always be used at the ends of cords or zips.
A hard knob of cotton-wool covered with buttonhole stitch
makes a good finish for a cord, or a circular piece of cardboard
covered with material and perhaps embroidered fits in quite
often with a stitched drawstring. A small tab of felt slipped
through the loop on a zip fastener and stitched down is often a
good finish (197). The really important thing is to make your
finishings fit in with the general scheme of the work.

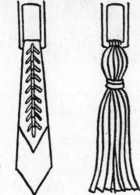

197

Fringes are another attractive finish for embroidery. The simplest fringe (198) is made by unravelling one set of threads of the material. If this method is used, start by drawing several threads the required distance from the edge and hemstitching along the inner edge. Then pull out the remaining threads. If necessary this fringe can be knotted afterwards (199).

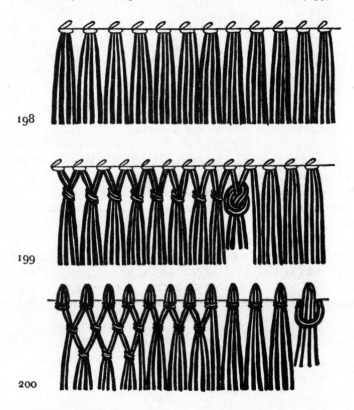

198

199

200

The other method (200) is to take groups of threads which should be twice as long as the length your fringe is to be. Fold the group of threads in half and pull the loop through the fabric a little way from the edge. Then pass the ends of the threads through the loop and pull it up to the edge of the material. These too may be knotted. Take care to see that all knots are tied in the same way. A second row of knots may be

tied by taking half the threads from one group and knotting
them with half from the next group.

Actual fastenings vary too. The ordinary buttonhole is
quite familiar. It should be large enough for the button to
slip through easily and without tugging. A buttonhole loop is
made by carrying a number of threads from one place to another
loosely to make a loop and then covering them with a close
buttonhole stitch (201). Make sure that the loop will slip easily
over the button.

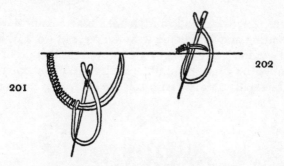

201   202

A buttonhole bar is made in the same way (202). Sometimes
a series of these bars worked at intervals will form a passage for
a cord as along the top of a drawstring bag. Loops made from
material should be inserted between two pieces of fabric, and
not stitched on by their ends. The strip of material forming the
loop may be machined or else hand-stitched round a piece of
piping cord.

Instead of having a button and loop to fasten a box, a stitched
loop can be fixed to the bottom edge and a cord sewn round the
lid, the long ends being threaded through the loop and tied in
a bow (203). Sometimes the cords of a bag are threaded through

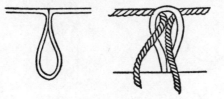

203

eyelets which are made in the following way (204): make a row
of running stitches round the place where the eyelet is to be and
then pierce the hole with a stiletto; oversew the edges tightly
and then pierce the hole once again.

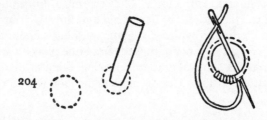

204

Buttons which are made and devised by the embroideress are
more exciting and in keeping with the piece of work which they
are to decorate. Even if they are utilitarian, there is no reason
for them to be dull and uninteresting. A plain linen button
stitched on with a star or with coloured thread is more exciting

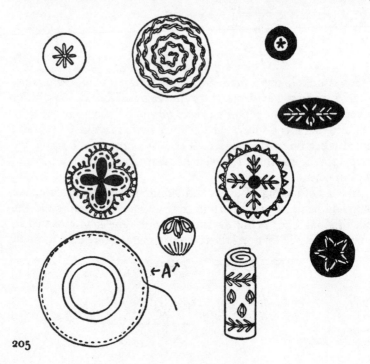

205

than one attached with a few haphazard stitches. Button moulds can be bought in the shops, and material from the embroidery used to cover them. But if these are not available a piece of stiff cardboard with a layer of cotton wadding over it serves very well as a button mould. This way is useful for sizes that cannot be bought. The button covering may be embroidered in many different ways to correspond with the article to which it is to be attached. If a patterned material has been used, a piece of the pattern is sometimes cut out to cover the button and form the basis for a tiny embroidered motif. If a button in the form of a knob is required, make a hard ball of cotton wadding and cover it with a circle of material gathered round the outside edge. If the material frays, the edges should be turned in before the gathering thread is put in. When pulled up, the circle should fit snugly round the button (205A).

Now a word about zips. The zip can be machined into the work according to instructions on the packet, but it can also be handstitched into a piece of embroidery and an embroidered stitch worked round it so that it forms part of the decoration on the piece of work as well as serving a useful purpose. Cushion-

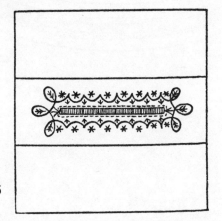

206

cases or nightdress-cases are often fastened by zips. The zip in the gusset of a cushion-case may be a beautiful piece of decoration. It is sometimes inserted into the middle of the cushion (206), and there again makes a decorative piece of work in

keeping with the whole.   To fix in a zip in this way, cut a slit
slightly smaller in length than the zip itself.   Turn in the edges
and tack them on to the zip, starting from the centre and working towards each end.   Clip the corners diagonally and turn
in the little triangular piece at each end and tack firmly in
place.   This is now ready for stitching either by hand or by
machine.   Sometimes it is wiser to machine the zip in first and
then work an embroidered border over the stitching.   If the
cushion-case has a gusset, the zip may be inserted in this and
form part of the decoration round the edge (207).   There is no
need for a zip or fastening of any kind to look ugly or out of
place if a little thought is given to the suitability and appro-
priateness of it, so that it makes for a harmonious whole, fitting
in with the piece of work without losing its functional value.

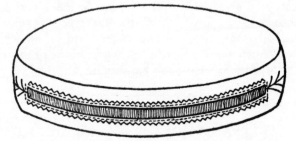

207

208 *Cushion with tassels and zip, and a design of loops and scallops,
showing two methods of working it. Try this out with thick thread
or wool on a coarse fabric*

SOME MORE WAYS OF USING
EMBROIDERY

IN this section you will find some measurements and methods of construction for several more articles. They are simple at the beginning and become progressively more difficult. The design is left to the embroideress herself, so that she can make use of the stitches and methods which have been discussed in previous sections. Finally there are some further suggestions for the applied use of embroidery, but without detailed instructions since the necessary details can be found in previous sections.

Felt Juliet Cap

This is very simple to make, consisting of six shapes either machined together on the wrong side or stitched with fishbone on the right side. If you use the machine remember to leave turnings right round. The cap in the diagram (209) was made of felt and each section was the same. Six copies of the design are necessary, and each is tacked on to a section. This cap was decorated with beads and sequins. If you choose this type of decoration see that the beads and sequins fit in with the design itself, and leave spaces for them when drawing it out. They must not be added as an afterthought, but must be incorporated into the pattern and be part of it. This is most important. Stitch the beads, etc., on to the work regularly, making them fit in with the embroidery stitches. This kind of work is only appropriate for articles which are not going to be washed and for those things which do not have a great deal of wear—evening bags, evening caps, jewel- and trinket-boxes, etc. The

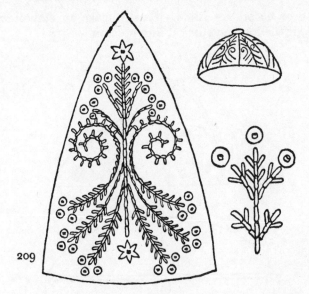

209

method of sewing on the sequins can be seen in diagram 210.
You will need a very fine needle and fine sewing cotton.   Single
sequins can be sewn on with a bead, but rows of them must be
stitched with an oversewing stitch, each sequin overlapping
the previous one so as to hide the stitch.   When you have
worked the embroidery on each section, stitch them together
carefully with fishbone, seeing that they are level at the bottom
and all meet at the top.   Make a silk lining to correspond,
machining the pieces together on the wrong side, and fit it
inside the cap.   Turn under the raw edge and finish off with a

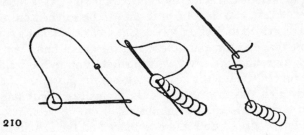

210

seaming or decorative stitch. Finally make an embroidered button for the top and stitch it into position.

Knitting-bag (211)

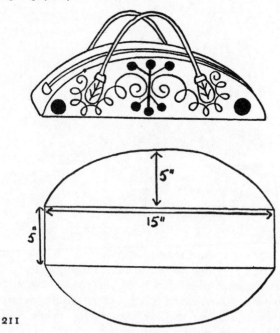

211

To make the knitting-bag you will need felt, tailor's canvas, lining, cotton wadding, four rings and some thick cord or string for the handles and a 14″ zip. Cut out the main shape and a strip 5″ wide and long enough to extend round the curved edge for the gusset. Make your design for the sides, not forgetting to include the holders for the handle rings, tack it on and work it. Make two handles with tabs to be stitched on to the sides as described in Section VII. Cut a piece of tailor's canvas the same shape as the main piece and the gusset but ¼″ smaller all the way round and invisibly slip stitch it on to the inside of the felt pieces. Cut a slit in the centre of the gusset to take the zip and stitch this in firmly. Make a small semi-circular tab at each end of the zip and also a small one to attach to the handle of the zip. Stitch these in place and then stitch in the

gusset, using a running, strettle or overcasting stitch. For
the lining I suggest machine quilting in some all-over pattern.
Cut a piece of material large enough for both the gusset and the
main bag part.   Tack it on to a layer of cotton wadding, and
after you have quilted it, cut out your pieces.   Machine them
together on the wrong side and then cut a slit in the gusset as
long as the zip.   Place the lining inside the bag, turn in the
edges along the sides of the zip and hem them down firmly.

Jewel-box (212)

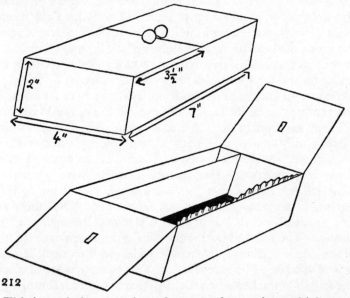

212

This is made in a number of rectangular sections which must
be cut accurately or the box will not fit together.   You will
need material for the outside, some for the lining, cotton
wadding, a small piece of narrow elastic for the pocket and some
very firm cardboard.   Cut out the card to the measurements in
the diagram; that is one piece for the base 4″ by 7″, two lids
3½″ by 4″, two short sides 2″ by 4″, two long sides 2″ by 7″ and an
additional long piece for the division inside.   This will need to
be slightly smaller than the long side of the box, as it must fit
inside.   Cut these same measurements out in tracing paper and
work out your design.   Cut pieces of material for the outside

of the box, allowing ¼″ turning all round.   This is not necessary
if the outer cover is to be felt.   Work the embroidery and press
each piece well.

Fold each piece of outer covering over the corresponding
piece of card and secure it on the other side with strips of sello-
tape.   Make sure that the material is drawn tightly over the
card.   If you wish the outside to be slightly padded, as well as
the inside, cut a piece of wadding the same size as the card and
fold your material over the two together, having the wadding
between the material and the card.   Next cut all the pieces for
the lining, again allowing ½″ extra all round.   Fold in the
extra ½″ right round, and after placing a piece of wadding on
the inside of the card, seam the edges of the lining and the outer
cover together neatly and with fine cotton.   Before putting the
lining on the lids make two small tabs of material by folding a
narrow strip and seaming down the side, and hem them one in
the centre of each lid lining.   These are to hold brooches and
are best sewn on before the box is assembled.   The hemming
stitches may be covered with an embroidery stitch such as
buttonhole.   Make the knobs for the top of the box and stitch
them into position.   The pocket is made with a strip of
material 12″ long and 3″ wide.   Turn in and hem down a
narrow hem on one long and two short sides.   The other long
side needs a deeper hem so that a slot may be made for the
elastic.   The finished pocket should reach not quite to the top
of the side.   Make the top hem ½″ wide and then work another
row of stitching ¼″ above this.   Take a narrow piece of elastic
the length of the box when slightly stretched, slot it through the
heading and secure it firmly at each end.   Run a gathering
thread along the bottom edge of the pocket and pull it up to the
length of the side.   Hem the bottom and two sides of the pocket
to the inside of one of the side pieces.   Next make the dividing
strip.   Pad the piece of card with wadding on both sides and
fold round it a piece of lining, seaming the edges together along
the bottom and sides.

All the pieces of the box are now ready to assemble.   Place
the dividing section between the two short sides, equidistant
from the ends, and catch stitch it to them at the top and
bottom.   Next seam the long sides to the short sides with

a fine but strong thread.   Then stitch the four sides on to
the base.   The lids are attached by tiny buttonhole bars
about $\frac{1}{4}''$ from each end.   They should move easily and rest on
the box sides when it is closed.   Additional pieces may be made
for the inside if you wish.   A small bag for special beads, for
instance, and little pads to fit the floors of the compartments.
These are attractive made in felt—two layers with wadding
between and stitched down at intervals as for a tea-cosy lining.
The edges look well if they are pinked.   It is essential that these
pads are really made to fit their compartments comfortably and
without folding.   Lastly a couched thread round the outside,
or a fine cord made and stitched over the seams, completes the
box.   When starting and finishing the couching thread, run it
in from inside the material so that the ends are covered and
there are no raw edges showing.

Sewing-box (213)

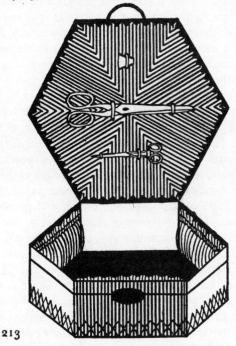

213

This is made in the same way as the jewel-box.   Each piece

is made separately and then they are all assembled. For this box you will need material for the outside, some for the lining and pockets, very firm and rigid card and some drawing-paper. Try an experiment with the colour when making this box. For instance the outside could have two or three colours, perhaps some plain and some striped—or one side may be a light colour and one a dark one with sections on the lid to correspond. The lining too may be exciting—a vivid contrast to the outside and also with a little embroidery on it to link up with the outside. First of all cut out in drawing-paper six side pieces, two lid and two base pieces. Cut out the shapes in the outside fabric, leaving $\frac{1}{2}''$ turning all round. If the lid is made in six separate sections as it is in the diagram, then each piece of fabric must be cut separately. Very carefully and accurately machine them together on the wrong side and press the seams flat. Tack each piece over its appropriate shape of paper as you would when doing patchwork. Then make your design and work it. The stitching may go right through the paper as it is not necessary to remove it at the end. In exactly the same way mount the pieces of lining and work any stitching that is needed. Make the pockets next, as you did for the jewel-box, making a slot for elastic and gathering them along the bottom edge. A decorative edge along the top would look attractive too.

The next stage is to complete the lid. For the lining of the lid make five narrow strips of material as for the brooch-holders in the jewel-box. These are to hold the large pair of scissors, the small pair of scissors (two to a pair), and the thimble. Try the strips round these objects first so that you can make them the exact size to ensure a good fit. Stitch these strips into position on the lid linings with a little embroidery round the joins. Cut the pieces of card to correspond with the parts of the box, and place the appropriate piece of card between its outside and inside cover and neatly seam round the edges with a fine needle and cotton. Next sew the pockets into position. The box is now ready to assemble. Stitch all the side pieces together and then stitch these on to the base. Finally attach the lid with small buttonholed hinges, and make a button and loop for a fastening. If necessary couch round the outside seams with another thread.

Perhaps then you could make the equipment to go inside—a small pincushion, needle-case and scissors holder to correspond with the outside colour scheme and embroidery. Instructions for making these articles may be found earlier in the book (pp. 26, 115). The pincushion may be varied by making a casing or narrow tube of material slotted with elastic and attached to the base of the pincushion. It can then be worn on the wrist. A differently shaped sewing-box could be made up on the same plan. For instance, an octagon would be quite a pleasing shape. Perhaps the side pieces could be different colours each with their own individual motif. You will also find illustrated (214) an oval sewing-box made on the same plan as the round trinket-box (p. 58). The pockets are box-pleated at the bottom and left free at the top, and handles have been added.

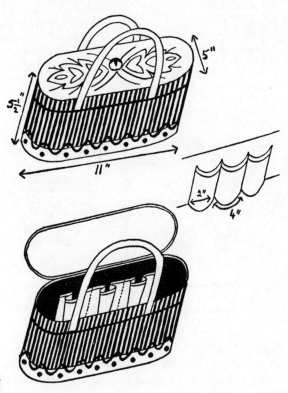

214

L

Quilted bedroom slippers

To make these slippers you will need a pair of wedge-heeled soles, which can be bought from a shop, some soft material such as crêpe de chine for the outside quilting, material for lining, tailor's canvas and a thin piping cord.   Leather soles also may be bought from the shop.   The pattern illustrated (215) is for size 4, but I advise cutting it in paper and making a fitting to your individual requirements before starting to make up the slippers.   Each square represents 1″.

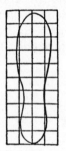
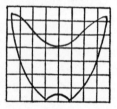
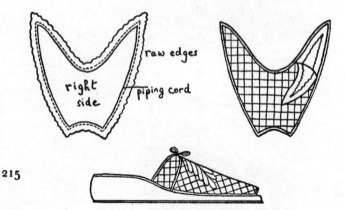

215

First of all cover the wedge and sole with material.   Cut a strip wide enough to extend on to the top and bottom of the sole and long enough to go right round, and stretch it tightly round the sole, joining the two ends at the inside instep. You will need to pleat the fabric on the top and bottom and stitch it firmly, but no pleats must show round the outside edge. Tack a piece of lining material on to a piece of wadding, having the size large enough to take the insides of the slipper fronts and the two inside soles. Quilt this piece of material all in one piece and then cut out the shapes for the fronts and soles of the slippers, taking care to allow a turning right round and seeing that the lines of quilting correspond exactly on each piece. Either machine or hand quilting may be used for this. Perhaps you may prefer a design of dots or crosses—it depends largely on the pattern of the material. Place the sole on the upper side of the wedge, turn in the edges right round and stitch very neatly.

Next prepare the tops of the slippers. These may be quilted too by machine or by hand. Perhaps you would prefer a quilted pattern on the tops. If this is so, draw it out first on a piece of paper and see that the design does not extend right to the edge. If you are having a special design, tack round the exact shape on your material before working it. This part of the slipper may be embroidered if you wish. When the stitchery is finished, cut out the shapes leaving $\frac{1}{2}''$ turning all round. Then cut out two slipper front pieces in tailor's canvas, this time to the exact size, and slip stitch them on to the wrong side of the lining pieces. Next cover sufficient narrow piping cord to go right round the slipper front and stitch it to the outside of the embroidered pieces. Join the piping at one of the corners. Fold the piping over on to the wrong side and then tack on the lining pieces, turning the edge in right round, and finally hem it on to the piping. This is now ready to put on to the sole. Pin it firmly into position and with strong thread stitch invisibly through the edge where the piping meets the upper on to the sole. A tiny bow of piping may be added to the front if desired. Lastly cut some thin leather soles to size and stick them on to the bottom of the slippers.

216 *Simple designs based on loops and scallops. Try out different stitches and some fillings*

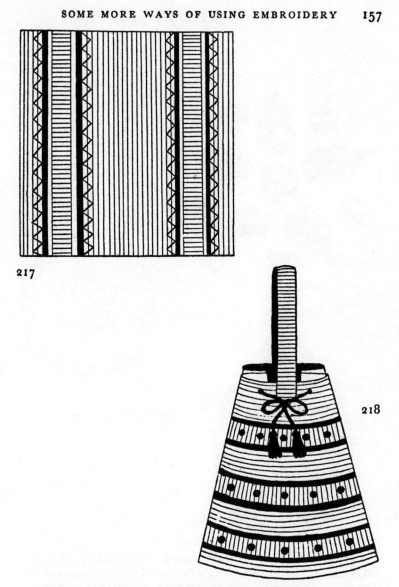

217 *Striped cushion with binding and hand embroidery or machine stitching*

218 *Striped bag made from straight piece of material on oval stiffened base.   Eyelets worked round top for cord*

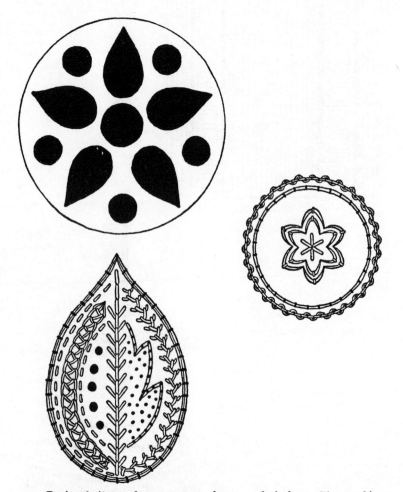

219 *Design built up from cut paper leaves and circles.   Try working this out in thick cotton on woollen material.   Work each leaf and circle differently, starting with the two illustrated*

220 *Design from cut paper shapes with the addition of lines.   Try it in felt appliqué and a fairly thick thread.   Suitable for cushion or chair pad*

221 *Design from simple cut paper stars with the addition of some
lines. Suitable for patchwork cushion—red and white, grey, white
and black, or blue and white—or for hanging wall pockets worked in
appliqué. Single stars may be used for a box lid or the front of a
needlecase*

222 *Cut paper shapes building up a complex bird.   Try this out in black and white in embroidery, or appliqué with the addition of some stitches*

223 *Round bag with alternating bands of needleweaving and embroidery. The part of the bag with the stitchery on can be stiffened inside with tailor's canvas if desired. Use a fairly coarse material and a thick thread*

224 *Cot cover with stripes of contrasting materials and animal shapes.*
Keep the shapes very simple and embroider each one differently. This
is suitable for appliqué too

INDEX

We have a wide range of books on embroidery, dressmaking and other needlecrafts—written by experts and attractively produced. If you would like details, please send a postcard for our free catalogue, mentioning this advertisement